AAT

Qualifications and Credit Framework (QCF)

AQ2013 (FA2014)
LEVEL 4 DIPLOMA IN ACCOUNTING

QUESTION BANK

Personal Tax

2014 Edition

For assessments from January 2015

Second edition August 2014
ISBN 9781 4727 09431

Previous edition August 2013
ISBN 9781 4727 03583

British Library Cataloguing-in-Publication Data
A catalogue record for this book is available from the British Library

Published by
BPP Learning Media Ltd
BPP House
Aldine Place
London W12 8AA

www.bpp.com/learningmedia

Printed in the United Kingdom by Martins of Berwick
Sea View Works
Spittal
Berwick-Upon-Tweed
TD15 1RS

> Your learning materials, published by BPP Learning Media Ltd, are printed on paper obtained from traceable, sustainable sources.

All our rights reserved. No part of this publication may be reproduced, stored in a retrieval system or transmitted, in any form or by any means, electronic, mechanical, photocopying, recording or otherwise, without the prior written permission of BPP Learning Media Ltd.

The contents of this book are intended as a guide and not for professional advice. Although every effort has been made to ensure that the contents of this book are correct at the time of going to press, BPP Learning Media makes no warranty that the information in this book is accurate or complete and accepts no liability for any loss or damaged suffered by any person acting or refraining from acting as a result of the material in this book.

We are grateful to the AAT for permission to reproduce the sample assessment(s). The answers to the sample assessment(s) have been published by the AAT. All other answers have been prepared by BPP Learning Media Ltd.

©
BPP Learning Media Ltd
2014

CONTENTS

A note about copyright	iv
Introduction	v
Approaching the assessment	vi

Question and Answer bank

Practice Tasks

	Questions	Answers
The tax framework	3	69
Taxable income	7	73
Calculation of income tax	13	81
Employment income	19	91
Property income	33	107
Payment of tax and tax administration	41	115
Chargeable gains	51	121
Share disposals	61	131
Principal private residence	65	135

Practice Assessments

	Questions	Answers
AAT AQ2013 Sample Assessment	139	153
BPP practice assessment 1	165	179
BPP practice assessment 2	191	209
BPP practice assessment 3	223	243
BPP practice assessment 4	257	275
BPP practice assessment 5	287	303

Taxation data   313

BPP note: Assessments under FA 2013 will cease to be available from 31 December 2014. Assessments under FA 2014 will be available from January 2015. This Text edition includes the provisions of FA 2014 and has been written specifically for students sitting AQ2013. Please ensure you check the date you intend to sit your assessment to ensure you are using the correct material.

A NOTE ABOUT COPYRIGHT

Dear Customer

What does the little © mean and why does it matter?

Your market-leading BPP books, course materials and e-learning materials do not write and update themselves. People write them on their own behalf or as employees of an organisation that invests in this activity. Copyright law protects their livelihoods. It does so by creating rights over the use of the content.

Breach of copyright is a form of theft – as well being a criminal offence in some jurisdictions, it is potentially a serious breach of professional ethics.

With current technology, things might seem a bit hazy but, basically, without the express permission of BPP Learning Media:

- Photocopying our materials is a breach of copyright.
- Scanning, ripcasting or conversion of our digital materials into different file formats, uploading them to Facebook or emailing them to your friends is a breach of copyright.

You can, of course, sell your books, in the form in which you have bought them – once you have finished with them. (Is this fair to your fellow students? We update for a reason). Please note the e-products are sold on a single user licence basis: we do not supply 'unlock' codes to people who have bought them secondhand.

And what about outside the UK? BPP Learning Media strives to make our materials available at prices students can afford by local printing arrangements, pricing policies and partnerships which are clearly listed on our website. A tiny minority ignore this and indulge in criminal activity by illegally photocopying our material or supporting organisations that do. If they act illegally and unethically in one area, can you really trust them?

INTRODUCTION

This is BPP Learning Media's AAT Question Bank for Personal Tax. It is part of a suite of ground-breaking resources produced by BPP Learning Media for the AAT's assessments under the Qualification and Credit Framework.

The Personal Tax assessment will be **computer assessed**. As well as being available in the traditional paper format, this **Question Bank is available in an online environment** containing tasks similar to those you will encounter in the AAT's testing environment. BPP Learning Media believe that the best way to practise for an online assessment is in an online environment. However, if you are unable to practise in the online environment you will find that all tasks in the paper Question Bank have been written in a style that is as close as possible to the style that you will be presented with in your online assessment.

This Question Bank has been written in conjunction with the BPP Text, and has been carefully designed to enable students to practise all of the learning outcomes and assessment criteria for the unit that makes up Personal Tax. It is fully up to date for Finance Act 2014 and reflects both the AAT's unit guide and the AAT sample assessments provided by the AAT.

This Question Bank contains these key features:

- Tasks corresponding to each chapter of the Text. Some tasks are designed for learning purposes, others are of assessment standard.
- The AAT's AQ2013 Sample Assessment and answers for Personal Tax and further BPP practice assessments.

The emphasis in all tasks and assessments is on the practical application of the skills acquired.

VAT

You may find tasks throughout this Question Bank that need you to calculate or be aware of a rate of VAT. This is stated at 20% in these examples and questions.

Introduction

APPROACHING THE ASSESSMENT

When you sit the assessment it is very important that you follow the on screen instructions. This means you need to carefully read the instructions, both on the introduction screens and during specific tasks.

When you access the assessment you should be presented with an introductory screen with information similar to that shown below (taken from the introductory screen from the AAT's AQ2013 sample assessments for Personal Tax).

> We have provided the following sample assessment to help you familiarise yourself with AAT's e-assessment environment. It is designed to demonstrate as many as possible of the question types you may find in a live assessment. It is not designed to be used on its own to determine whether you are ready for a live assessment.
>
> You should attempt and aim to complete EVERY task.
> Each task is independent. You will not need to refer to your answers to previous tasks.
> Read every task carefully to make sure you understand what is required.
>
> Please note that in this sample test only your responses to tasks 1, 2, 3, 4, 5, 9 and 11 are marked. Equivalents of tasks 6, 7, 8 and 10 will be human marked in the live assessment.
>
> Where the date is relevant, it is given in the task data.
> Both minus signs and brackets can be used to indicate negative numbers UNLESS task instructions say otherwise.
> You must use a full stop to indicate a decimal point - for example, write 100.57 NOT 100,57 or 100 57
>
> You may use a comma to indicate a number in the thousands, but you don't have to.
> For example, 10000 and 10,000 are both OK.
>
> Other indicators are not compatible with the computer-marked system.
>
> Tax data is provided in this assessment. The data has been grouped into two parts to make it easier to display. You can access the data at any point by clicking on the buttons found in every task. The buttons will appear at the top of each task, and look like this:
>
> [i] Taxation data 1   [i] Taxation data 2
>
> When you click on a button, the table will appear in a pop-up window. You can then move or close the window. When you move on to a new task, you will have to re-open a window to see the data again.
>
> The taxation data is also available below, in this introduction, and can be accessed at any time during the assessment by clicking on the introduction button on the bottom left of the assessment window.

The actual instructions will vary depending on the subject you are studying for. It is very important you read the instructions on the introductory screen and apply them in the assessment. You don't want to lose marks when you know the correct answer just because you have not entered it in the right format.

In general, the rules set out in the AAT sample assessments for the subject you are studying for will apply in the real assessment, but you should again read the information on this screen in the real assessment carefully just to make sure.

A full stop is needed to indicate a decimal point. We would recommend using minus signs to indicate negative numbers and leaving out the comma signs to indicate thousands, as this results in a lower number of key strokes and less margin for error when working under time pressure. Having said that, you can use whatever is easiest for you as long as you operate within the rules set out for your particular assessment.

You have to show competence in all sections of assessments and you should therefore complete all of the tasks. Don't leave questions unanswered.

In some assessments written or complex tasks may be human marked. In this case you are given a blank space or table to enter your answer into. You are told in the assessments which tasks these are.

If these involve calculations, it is a good idea to decide in advance how you are going to lay out your answers to such tasks by practising answering them on a word document, and certainly you should try all such tasks in this question bank and in the AAT's environment using the sample/practice assessments.

When asked to fill in tables, or gaps, never leave any blank even if you are unsure of the answer. Fill in your best estimate or enter a zero.

Note that for some assessments where there is a lot of scenario information or tables of data provided (eg tax tables), you may need to access these via 'pop-ups'. Instructions will be provided on how you can bring up the necessary data during the assessment.

Finally, take note of any task specific instructions once you are in the assessment. For example you may be asked to enter a date in a certain format or to enter a number to a certain number of decimal places.

Remember you can practise the BPP questions in this question bank in an online environment on our dedicated AAT Online page. On the same page is a link to the current AAT Sample Assessments as well.

If you have any comments about this book, please email Ianblackmore@bpp.com or write to Ian Blackmore, AAT Range Manager, BPP Learning Media Ltd, BPP House, Aldine Place, London W12 8AA.

Introduction

SPECIFIC TOPIC LIST

The practice tasks are grouped according to the main topics assessed in Personal Tax. This table gives you a list of tasks dealing with specific topics to enable you to focus your task practice.

Topic	Practice tasks
Legislation and procedures	1.1, 1.2, 1.3
Duties and responsibilities of a tax practitioner	1.4, 1.5, 1.6, 1.7, 1.8
Types of income (non-savings, savings, dividend and exempt income)	2.1, 2.2, 2.4, 2.12, 2.13, 2.14
Calculation of taxable income	2.5, 2.6
Personal & age allowances	2.3, 2.7, 2.8, 2.9, 2.10, 2.11, 3.11
Income tax liability & payable	3.1, 3.2, 3.3, 3.4, 3.5, 3.6, 3.7, 3.8, 3.9, 3.10
Employed versus self-employed	4.1, 4.2
Car, fuel & van benefits	4.6, 4.7, 4.8, 4.9, 4.10, 4.26
Other employment benefits	4.11, 4.12, 4.13, 4.14, 4.15, 4.16, 4.17, 4.18, 4.19, 4.21
Allowable deductions from employment income	4.18, 4.22, 4.23, 4.24, 4.25
Calculation of employment income	4.3, 4.4, 4.5, 4.20
Employment tax return page	4.27
Calculation of property income	5.1, 5.2, 5.3, 5.4, 5.5, 5.6, 5.11, 5.13
Property income loss relief	5.7
Furnished holiday lets	5.8, 5.9, 5.10, 5.12, 5.14
Property income tax return pages	5.15
Filing date & payment of tax	6.1, 6.2, 6.9, 7.10
Record keeping	6.3
Penalties & interest	6.4, 6.5, 6.6, 6.7, 6.8
Chargeable disposals	7.1, 7.2, 7.3
Calculation of gains for individuals	7.4, 7.9, 7.12, 7.13
Capital losses	7.11, 7.14, 7.15
Capital gains tax payable	7.5, 7.6, 7.7, 7.8
Chattels	7.18, 7.19, 7.20, 7.21, 7.22
Connected persons	7.16, 7.17
Capital gains tax return pages	7.23
Share disposals	8.1, 8.2, 8.3, 8.4
Principal private residence relief	9.1, 9.2

Question bank

Question bank

Question bank

The tax framework

Task 1.1

The tax year 2014/15 runs from: (insert dates as xx/xx/xxxx)

6/4/2014

until

5/4/2015

Task 1.2

Tick to show whether the following statement is True or False.

Detailed regulations relating to tax law are contained in Statutory Instruments.

	✓
True	✓
False	

Task 1.3

Tick to show who the UK tax system is administered by.

	✓
Parliament	
Her Majesty's Revenue & Customs (HMRC)	✓
Serious Organised Crime Agency (SOCA)	
HM Customs & Excise	

Question bank

Task 1.4

If you are employed by a firm of accountants, and suspect that one of your clients may be engaged in money laundering, whom should you inform about your suspicions?

	✓
HMRC	
Your firm's Money Laundering Reporting Officer	✓
Serious Organised Crime Agency	
Tax Tribunal	

Task 1.5

This style of task is human marked in the live assessment.

One of your clients has expressed concern that his personal tax information may be disclosed to members of his family, who are also clients of your firm. He feels that this would compromise his right to privacy in his personal affairs.

Write a note responding to this concern.

Question bank

Task 1.6

Tick to show in which TWO of the following situations an accountant is able to disclose information about a client without their permission.

	✓
If the client is unwell and unable to respond to HMRC	
If money laundering is suspected	✓
Where it would be illegal not to disclose the information	✓
If the information is requested from a 'connected person'	

Task 1.7

The five fundamental principles on professional ethics for AAT members are:

Use the letters in the left column as a guide.

I	Integrity
O	Objectivity
Pc and dc	Professional competence + due care
C	Confidentiality
Pb	Professional behaviour

Task 1.8

Tick to show who you should inform about your suspicions if you are a sole practitioner, and suspect that one of your clients may be engaged in money laundering.

	✓
HMRC	
Another firm's Money Laundering Reporting Officer	
Serious Organised Crime Agency	✓
Tax Tribunal	

Question bank

Taxable income

Task 2.1

For each of the following sources of income, indicate whether it is non-savings income, savings income or dividend income by ticking the relevant box:

	Non-savings income	Savings income	Dividend income
Trading income	☐	☐	☐
Dividend received from a company	☐	☐	☐
Property income	☐	☐	☐
Building society interest	☐	☐	☐
Bank interest	☐	☐	☐
Pension income	☐	☐	☐
Employment income	☐	☐	☐
Interest from government stock ('gilts')	☐	☐	☐

Task 2.2

Olive received the following income in 2014/15.

Show the amount of income that she should enter on her tax return. If the income is exempt, enter 0.

(a) Bank account interest £160

£ ☐

(b) Premium bond prize £100

£ ☐

(c) Dividends received £540

£ ☐

Task 2.3

Bob was born in April 1944. His net income for 2014/15 is £27,800.

The age allowance Bob is entitled to for 2014/15 is:

£	

Task 2.4

For each of the following interest payments, indicate whether they are received gross, net of basic rate tax or are exempt from income tax by ticking the relevant box:

	Gross	Net	Exempt
Interest on NS&I savings certificate	☐	☐	☐
Bank interest	☐	☐	☐
Interest on NS&I investment account	☐	☐	☐
Interest on (new) individual savings account	☐	☐	☐
Interest on NS&I Direct Saver account	☐	☐	☐
Building society interest	☐	☐	☐
Interest from government stock ('gilts')	☐	☐	☐

Task 2.5

You act for Jonty, who was born in July 1969. The following information is relevant for the year ended 5 April 2015:

(1) His salary was £38,130.

(2) His other income received was:

		£
	38,130	
Building society interest	$\frac{100}{80}$ × 80 = 100	80
Dividends	$\frac{100}{90}$ × 63 = 70	63
	38,300	
	− 10,000	

Jonty's taxable income for 2014/15 is:

£	28,300

Question bank

Task 2.6

Mr Betteredge has the following income for 2014/15:

	£
Salary for the year to 5 April 2015	15,065
Interest received (cash received shown):	
National Westminster Bank plc	457
NISA account	180
Nationwide Building Society account	400

Using the proforma layout provided, prepare a schedule of income for 2014/15, clearly showing the distinction between non-savings and savings income. If income is exempt, enter 0. Mr Betteredge's personal allowance should be deducted as appropriate. Fill in ALL the unshaded boxes, and add a 0 (zero) if necessary.

	Non-savings income £	Savings income £	Total £
Earnings	15,065		
Bank deposit interest		571.25	
Building society interest		500	
NISA interest		0	
Net income	15,065	1,071.25	16,136.25
Less personal allowance	10,000		
Taxable income	5,065	1,071.25	6,136.22

Task 2.7

Hayley receives employment income of £95,000, bank interest of £1,600 and dividends of £4,500 in 2014/15.

(1) Hayley's net income for 2014/15 is:

£ 102,000

(2) The personal allowance that Hayley is entitled to for 2014/15 is:

£ 9,000

Question bank

Task 2.8

Max has net income of £115,000 for 2014/15. He made Gift Aid donations of £4,000 (gross) during the year.

Max's personal allowance for 2014/15 is:

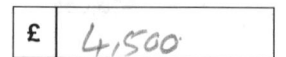

£ 4,500

Task 2.9

Gavin was born in September 1932. In 2014/15, he receives pension income of £19,000, bank interest of £2,000 and dividends of £5,400.

(1) **Gavin's net income for 2014/15 is:**

£ 27,500

(2) **The age allowance that Gavin is entitled to for 2014/15 is:**

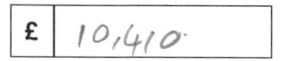

£ 10,410

Task 2.10

Sue was born in January 1938. In 2014/15, she receives pension income of £17,000, bank interest of £3,000 and dividends of £6,300.

(1) **Sue's net income for 2014/15 is:**

£

(2) **The age allowance that Sue is entitled to for 2014/15 is:**

£

Task 2.11

Ron was born in 1946. In 2014/15, he receives pension income of £33,000. He makes a Gift Aid donation of £1,500 (gross) in December 2014.

The age allowance that Ron is entitled to for 2014/15 is:

£

Task 2.12

From 1 July 2014 the maximum an individual can invest for the tax year in an NISA is:

£ ☐

Task 2.13

Tick to show whether the following statement is True or False.

Scholarships and educational grants are exempt as income of the student.

	✓
True	
False	

Task 2.14

Tick to show whether the following statement is True or False.

Damages received for an injury at work are only sometimes exempt from income tax, whereas damages paid on death are always exempt from income tax.

	✓
True	
False	

Question bank

Calculation of income tax

Task 3.1

Guy receives bank interest of £7,500 in 2014/15.

Calculate the income tax liability on the bank interest ONLY assuming he has other non-savings income (net of personal allowance) of:

(1) £1,000 (show whole pounds only)

£ ☐

(2) £30,000 (show whole pounds only)

£ ☐

Task 3.2

Holly is a higher rate taxpayer and receives a dividend of £5,913 in December 2014.

(1) **The tax credit attached to this dividend is:**

£ ☐

(2) **The rate of tax Holly will pay on this dividend (ignoring the effect of the tax credit) is:**

☐ %

Task 3.3

You act for Deidre Watkins. Deidre was born in 1959 and has the following taxable income for 2014/15:

Non-savings income £14,700

Savings income £2,176

Dividend income £1,766

Question bank

Calculate Deidre's tax liability (show whole pounds only) on each source of income for 2014/15 as follows:

(1) **Non-savings income:**

£ [   ]

(2) **Savings income:**

£ [   ]

(3) **Dividend income:**

£ [   ]

Task 3.4

Tony is a higher rate taxpayer and makes a Gift Aid donation of £6,000 in December 2014.

Tick to show the amount of Tony's basic rate band in 2014/15.

	✓
£37,865	
£31,865	
£39,365	
£36,665	

Task 3.5

Katy is an additional rate taxpayer and makes a Gift Aid donation of £4,000 in June 2014.

(1) **Katy's basic rate band for 2014/15 is:**

£ [   ]

(2) **Katy's higher rate band for 2014/15 is:**

£ [   ]

(3) **Katy's additional rate threshold for 2014/15 is:**

£ [   ]

Question bank

Task 3.6

Rachel (born in 1966) received £12,000 bank interest in 2014/15. This is her only income.

Rachel's income tax liability for 2014/15 is:

£ [   ]

Task 3.7

Richard has taxable non-savings income of £58,525 in 2014/15. He made pension contributions to his personal pension scheme of £10,800 during the year. Tax of £9,700 was deducted under the PAYE system.

Richard's income tax payable for 2014/15 is:

£ [   ]

Task 3.8

John Smith has the following income and outgoings for the tax year 2014/15:

	£
Salary (£8,500 tax deducted under PAYE)	50,000
Interest on a deposit account with the Scotia Bank	800
Donation under the Gift Aid scheme made on 1 September 2014	2,400
Dividends received on UK shares	900

(1) Using the proforma layout provided, prepare a schedule of income for 2014/15, clearly showing the distinction between non-savings, savings and dividend income. Fill in all the unshaded boxes. If an answer is zero input 0.

	Non-savings income £	Savings income £	Dividend income £	Total £
Salary	50,000	0	0	
Dividend	0	0	1000	
Bank deposit interest	0	1000	0	
Net income	50,000	1000	1000	52,000
Less personal allowance	10000	0	0	(10,000)
Taxable income	40,000	1000	1000	42,000

15

Question bank

(2) **John's income tax liability for 2014/15 is:**

£ ☐

(3) **John's income tax payable for 2014/15 is:**

£ ☐

Task 3.9

Jean Brown has the following income and outgoings for the tax year 2014/15:

	£
Salary (£48,500 tax deducted under PAYE)	155,000
Interest on a bank deposit account	2,400
Personal pension contribution	8,000
Dividends received on UK shares	4,500

(1) Using the proforma layout provided, prepare a schedule of income for 2014/15, clearly showing the distinction between non-savings, savings and dividend income. Fill in all the unshaded boxes. If an answer is zero input 0.

	Non-savings income £	Savings income £	Dividend income £	Total £
Salary				
Dividend				
Bank deposit interest				
Net income				
Less personal allowance				
Taxable income				

(2) **Jean's income tax liability for 2014/15 is:**

£ ☐

(3) **Jean's income tax payable for 2014/15 is:**

£ ☐

Task 3.10

This style of task is human marked in the live assessment.

During 2014/15 Joshua, who was born in 1944, has income as follows:

Pension income £9,200
Bank interest received £4,300
Dividends received £13,500

Joshua made a Gift Aid donation of £1,500 in July 2014.

Calculate Joshua's total income tax liability for 2014/15, using the table given below. Show your answer in whole pounds.

Task 3.11

During 2014/15 Amanda, who was born in February 1925, had pension income of £24,000. She also received dividends of £3,555. Amanda made a payment to charity under Gift Aid of £304 in December 2014.

What is Amanda's age allowance for 2014/15?

£ [ ]

Question bank

Employment income

Task 4.1

Show whether the following statement is True or False.

An employee has a contract for services.

	✓
True	
False	✓

Task 4.2

Peter undertakes some work for XYZ plc.

Tick which of the following factors would indicate that he either has a contract of service with XYZ plc or a contract for services.

Factor	Contract of service	Contract for services
Peter is entitled to paid holidays	✓	
Peter hires his own helpers		✓
Peter takes substantial financial risks when undertaking work for XYZ plc	✓	
Peter does not have to rectify mistakes in his work at his own expense		✓

Task 4.3

Emma is employed as a retail salesperson and provides you with the following information about money she has received from her employer:

(a) Monthly salary of £2,000 paid on the first of each month until September 2014, with a 2% increase starting from 1 October 2014

(b) Commission of £1,000 earned during a special sales event in March 2015, paid with the May 2015 salary

(c) Employer's contribution of 5% of salary on 31 March 2015 to company's occupational pension scheme

(d) Bonus of £1,200 received 30 April 2014, based on company's accounting profit for the year ended 31 March 2014

Question bank

For each item, show the amount that will be taxable in 2014/15:

Use whole numbers, and if the answer is zero, write 0

Item	£
Salary	24,250
Commission	0
Employer's pension contribution	0
Bonus	1200

Task 4.4

Show whether the following statement is True or False.

Tips received by a tour guide from customers are not earnings

True	
False	✓

Task 4.5

A director of a company is entitled to a bonus for her employer's year ended 31 December 2014. The bonus is determined on 30 November 2014, credited to her director's account on 20 December 2014 and is actually paid to her on 6 January 2015.

The date of receipt of the bonus for employment income purposes is: (insert date as xx/xx/xxxx)

[   ]

Task 4.6

Mo was provided with a petrol engine car by her employer on 6 August 2014. The car cost the employer £13,500 and the list price of the car was £15,000. The car's CO_2 emissions were 198g/km.

(1) The cost of the car in the taxable benefit computation is:

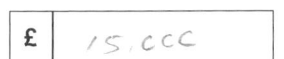

£ 15,000

(2) The percentage used in the taxable benefit computation is:

32 %

(3) The taxable benefit on the provision of the car is:

£ 3,200   8 months.

Task 4.7

Frank was provided with a new diesel engine car with a list price of £25,000 on 6 June 2014. The firm paid for all fuel (£2,300) without requiring any payment by Frank for fuel for private use. However, he was required to pay the firm £35 per month for the private use of the car itself. The car has CO_2 emissions of 173g/km.

(1) The taxable benefit on the provision of the car is:

£

(2) The taxable benefit on the provision of fuel is:

£

Question bank

Task 4.8

Julian is provided with a company car for business and private use throughout 2014/15. The car had a list price of £11,500 when bought new in December 2013 although the company paid £10,000 for the car after a dealer discount. It has a diesel engine, with CO_2 emissions of 70g/km. The company pays for all running costs, including all fuel. Julian does not make any contribution for his private use of the car.

(1) The cost of the car in the taxable benefit computation is:

£ [ ]

(2) The percentage used in the taxable benefit computation is:

[ ] %

(3) The taxable benefit in respect of the provision of fuel for private use is:

£ [ ]

Task 4.9

Sarah works for XXM plc, and is provided with a company car for business and private use throughout 2014/15.

The car has a diesel engine with CO_2 emissions of 209g/km. It has a list price of £57,000. Sarah agreed to make a capital contribution of £6,000 towards the cost of the car. The company pays for all running costs, including all fuel. Sarah pays £50 a month towards the cost of private fuel – the actual cost of private fuel is about £90 a month.

(1) Tick to show which percentage is used in the taxable benefit computation.

	✓
25	
35	
37	
34	

(2) The taxable benefit in respect of the provision of the car is:

£ [ ]

(3) The taxable benefit in respect of the provision of the fuel for private use is:

£ [ ]

Task 4.10

Francine is employed by Bale plc as a delivery driver and is supplied with a van, which she parks overnight at home. She uses the van to drive to the company's depot to pick up packages but otherwise is not allowed to use the van for her own private purposes. The company provides fuel for the van. The cost of fuel for driving the van from her home to the depot is £500 for 2014/15.

Tick to show the taxable benefit for Francine in respect of the van for 2014/15.

	✓
£3,090	
£3,671	
£3,590	
nil	

Task 4.11

A camera costing £200 is bought by an employer for the private use by an employee on 6 April 2013. The camera is purchased by the employee for £50 on 6 April 2014, when its market value is £120.

The taxable benefit for 2014/15 is:

£ ⬚

Task 4.12

On 6 April 2014 an employer made a loan of £50,000 to an employee. The employee repaid £30,000 on 6 December 2014. The remaining £20,000 was outstanding at 5 April 2015. Interest paid during the year was £1,000. The official rate of interest was 3.25% throughout 2014/15.

(1) **Using the average method, the taxable benefit for 2014/15 is:**

£ ⬚

(2) **Using the alternative method, the taxable benefit for 2014/15 is:**

£ ⬚

Question bank

Task 4.13

Tick to show whether the following statement is true or false.

If a loan of £7,000 to an employee is written-off and this is the only loan to the employee by the employer, there is no taxable benefit.

True	
False	✓

Task 4.14

(1) Vimal, who earns £30,000 a year, is given the use of a new television, costing £1,000, by his employer on 1 January 2013. Vimal subsequently buys the television from his employer for £100 on 1 January 2015 when it is worth £300.

The taxable benefit for 2014/15 is:

£ [   ]

(2) The television is used to keep Vimal entertained when living at 3 Sims Court, London EC1, a flat provided by his employer. The flat cost £120,000, five years ago when Vimal moved in, but due to a slump in property prices is now only worth £90,000. It has an annual value of £3,000. The official rate of interest is 3.25%.

The taxable benefit for 2014/15 is:

£ [   ]

Task 4.15

Giles receives a salary of £25,000 and has received the following benefits from his employer throughout 2014/15:

(1) Free medical insurance – the cost to the company is £385 per annum, although if Giles had taken this out privately he would have to pay £525.
(2) £55 per week of child care vouchers to be used towards the provision of creche facilities for his child who attends a private nursery.
(3) A newspaper allowance of £20 per month.

Giles receives no income other than employment income.

The total taxable benefits for 2014/15 are:

£ [   ]

Question bank

Task 4.16

Rita, a fashion designer for Daring Designs Ltd, was relocated from London to Manchester on 6 April 2014. Her annual salary is £48,000. She was immediately provided with a house with an annual value of £4,000, for which her employer paid an annual rent of £3,500. Rita was reimbursed relevant relocation expenditure of £12,000. Rita's employer provided ancillary services for the house in 2014/15 as follows:

	£
Electricity	700
Gas	1,200
Water	500
Council tax	1,300
Property repairs	3,500

The house had been furnished by Daring Designs Ltd immediately prior to Rita's occupation, at a cost of £30,000. On 6 October 2014 Rita bought all of the furniture from Daring Designs Ltd for £20,000 when its market value was £25,000.

Daring Designs Limited had made an interest-free loan to Rita in 2013 of £10,000. No part of the loan has been repaid. Assume the official rate of interest is 3.25%.

(1) **The taxable benefit arising in respect of the accommodation provided for Rita in 2014/15 and purchase of the furniture is:**

£ _____

(2) **The taxable benefit arising in respect of the relocation expenses is:**

£ _____

(3) **The taxable benefit arising in respect of the interest-free loan in 2014/15 is:**

£ _____

Annual value £4,000
cost of service £3,700 + £3,500
private use of furniture £30,000 × 20% × 6/12 = £3,000
purchase asset (£30,000 − £3,000) = £27,000 or £25,000 (take higher)
£27,000 − £20,000 = £7,000 (B i K)

Task 4.17

Jon's employer provided him with a flat throughout 2014/15. The employer had bought the flat for £97,000 on 1 April 2012. The annual value of the flat is £800. Jon pays £100 a month to his employer for the use of the flat.

Tick to show the total taxable accommodation benefit for 2014/15.

	✓
£800	
£1,515	
£315	
£715	

Task 4.18

Petra uses her own car for business travel and her employer reimburses her 35p per mile. In 2014/15 Petra drove 13,000 business miles.

Tick to show what is Petra's taxable benefit or allowable expense in respect of the business mileage.

	✓
Taxable benefit of £700	
Allowable expense of £700	
Allowable expense of £1,300	
Taxable benefit of £4,550	

Task 4.19

For an employee on an annual salary of £27,000, tick for each of the following benefits whether they would be taxable or exempt in 2014/15:

Item	Taxable	Exempt
Interest on loan of £2,000 (only loan provided)		☑
Removal costs of £6,000		☑
Use of pool car		☑
Reimbursement of business expenses under a dispensation		☑
One staff party costing £100 per head		☑
Accommodation provided to employee who is not required to live in it for the performance of employment	☑	
Provision of parking space at work		☑
Additional costs of home-working of £4 per week		☑
Long service award of £800 for 22 years service		☑
Accommodation provided to a caretaker for proper performance of his employment duties		☑
Work related training		☑
Provision of second mobile phone	☑	

Question bank

Task 4.20

Selina is employed by JKL Ltd. She gives you with the following information about money she has received from her employer, and expenditure that she has incurred in relation to her employment in 2014/15:

(a) Annual salary £30,000
(b) Reimbursed business expenses of £600 – HMRC has agreed a dispensation
(c) Employee's contribution of 8% of salary to company's occupational pension scheme
(d) Membership of professional body of £150 paid by Selina
(e) Membership of fitness club of £300 paid by Selina – she often uses the club to meet new clients
(f) £50 donation to charity each month under the payroll deduction scheme
(g) £1,500 expenditure on smart clothes to wear to client meetings

Using the proforma layout provided, compute Selina's employment income for 2014/15. If an expense is not allowable enter 0. Both brackets and minus signs can be used to indicate negative numbers (the expenses). Fill in all of the unshaded boxes.

		£
Salary		30,000
Less allowable expenses:		
	reimbursed expenses	0
	pension contribution	(2,400)
	professional body membership	(150)
	fitness club membership	0
	charitable donation	(600)
	clothing	0
Employment income 2014/15		26,850

Task 4.21

Lewis is required by his employer to move from Truro to Manchester.

The maximum amount of relocation expenses that his employer can pay without a taxable benefit arising is:

£ ☐

Question bank

Task 4.22

In 2014/15 Dave earns £20,000 a year in his employment with BCD plc, and also receives dividend income of £6,300 from the company.

Tick to show the maximum pension contribution that Dave can make in 2014/15, on which he can obtain tax relief.

	✓
£3,600	
£20,000	
£26,300	
£27,000	

Task 4.23

Zara works for KJ Ltd. She incurs the following travelling expenses in 2014/15:

	£
Travel from her home in Preston to her workplace in Manchester	1,500
Travel to meet clients	300
Travel from her home in Preston to a temporary workplace in Birmingham (temporary period is 18 months)	1,800

Zara's qualifying travel expenses for 2014/15 are:

£ ☐

Task 4.24

Tick to show how the payroll deduction scheme works.

	✓
The employer deducts the contribution after calculating income tax under PAYE.	
The employer deducts basic rate tax from the contribution and the employee gets higher rate relief by extending the basic rate band in the tax computation.	
The employer deducts the contribution before calculating income tax under PAYE.	
The employer deducts basic rate tax from the contribution and there is no higher rate tax relief.	

Task 4.25

Tick to show how the occupational pension scheme works.

	✓
The pension contribution is paid net of basic rate tax, and higher rate tax relief is obtained by extending the basic rate band.	
The contribution is deducted from employment income as an allowable expense before tax is calculated under PAYE.	

Task 4.26

This style of task is human marked in the live assessment.

You have received the following email from your client Martin Wilkes:

From:	MartinWilkes@boxmail.net
To:	AATStudent@boxmail.net
Sent:	12 March 2015 10:24
Subject:	Car

I have just received a promotion, and my employer is offering me a company car for business and personal use from 6 April 2015. My employer is getting a good deal on the car because I looked up the list price, which is £18,000, but they are only paying £14,000 after a discount from the dealer. I also noted that the car has CO_2 emissions of 173 g/km.

My employer will pay all the running costs of the car and will also provide all the fuel. I will pay £20 a month towards private fuel, but I think that my actual private fuel used would cost about £50.

Can you please explain all of the taxation aspects of the provision of this car as a taxable benefit? Is there any other information that you need to know?

Thanks,
Martin Wilkes

Reply to Martin's email, explaining to him the various taxation aspects that can apply to the provision of the car. Assume rates stay unchanged for future years.

From:	AATStudent@boxmail.net
To:	MartinWilkes@boxmail.net
Sent:	14 March 2015 12:29
Subject:	Car

Task 4.27

Your client, Jill Gilks, is employed by Beata plc. She has given you the following information about her employment:

Annual salary £60,000

Tax taken off pay £13,900

Company car – taxable benefit £5,200

Fuel benefit – taxable benefit £2,000

Expenses payments received £2,250 – this covers the exact amount spent by Jill on business travel. There is no dispensation agreed with HMRC

Professional subscription (paid by Jill) £225

Use this information to complete the Employment Page, which follows.

Question bank

HM Revenue & Customs

Employment
Tax year 6 April 2014 to 5 April 2015

Your name

Your unique taxpayer reference (UTR)

Complete an *Employment* page for each employment or directorship

1. Pay from this employment - the total from your P45 or P60 - before tax was taken off

2. UK tax taken off pay in box 1

3. Tips and other payments not on your P60 - *read page EN 3 of the notes*

4. PAYE tax reference of your employer (on your P45/P60)

5. Your employer's name

6. If you were a company director, put 'X' in the box

7. And, if the company was a close company, put 'X' in the box

8. If you are a part-time teacher in England or Wales and are on the Repayment of Teachers' Loans Scheme for this employment, put 'X' in the box

Benefits from your employment - use your form P11D (or equivalent information)

9. Company cars and vans - *the total 'cash equivalent' amount*

10. Fuel for company cars and vans - *the total 'cash equivalent' amount*

11. Private medical and dental insurance - *the total 'cash equivalent' amount*

12. Vouchers, credit cards and excess mileage allowance

13. Goods and other assets provided by your employer - *the total value or amount*

14. Accommodation provided by your employer - *the total value or amount*

15. Other benefits (including interest-free and low interest loans) - *the total 'cash equivalent' amount*

16. Expenses payments received and balancing charges

Employment expenses

17. Business travel and subsistence expenses

18. Fixed deductions for expenses

19. Professional fees and subscriptions

20. Other expenses and capital allowances

Shares schemes, employment lump sums, compensation, deductions and Seafarers' Earnings Deduction are on the *Additional information* pages enclosed in the tax return pack

SA102 2014   Tax return: Employment: Page E 1   HMRC 12/13

Property income

Task 5.1

Simran rents out a furnished house from 1 July 2014. The rent is £500 per month, payable on the first day of each month. She incurs the following costs relating to the rental:

	£
Electricity for 1 July 2014 to 31 March 2015	1,200
Water rates for 1 July 2014 to 31 March 2015	500
Insurance for 1 July 2014 to 30 June 2015	360

Simran claims the wear and tear allowance.

Tick to show what Simran's property income for 2014/15 is.

	✓
£2,080	
£1,990	
£2,040	
£2,130	

Task 5.2

Julie received the following property income during 2014/15:

(1) Annual rental of £6,300 (payable in advance) from a furnished flat first let on 6 August 2014. Allowable expenses of £660 relate to the let period. The tenant is responsible for paying water rates and council tax.

(2) £3,500 from letting a furnished room in her own home.

Julie claims the wear and tear allowance.

What amount of taxable property income does Julie have for 2014/15?

£ [ ]

Task 5.3

Zelda lets out a house. Her accrued income and allowable expenses are as follows:

	Income £	Expenses £
2012/13	6,000	10,000
2013/14	8,000	5,500
2014/15	10,000	4,000

Zelda's property income for 2014/15 is:

£ ☐

Task 5.4

On 1 October 2014 Nitin buys a badly dilapidated house for £350,000. During October 2014, he spends £40,000 on making the house habitable. He lets it furnished for £3,600 a month from 1 November 2014, but the tenant leaves on 31 January 2015. A new tenant moves in on 1 March 2015, paying £4,000 a month rent.

Water rates are £195 for the period 1 October 2014 to 31 March 2015, payable by Nitin. He also pays buildings insurance of £440 for the period from 1 October 2014 to 31 August 2015. He financed the purchase of £350,000 with a bank loan at 5% interest.

Nitin claims the wear and tear allowance. He spends £10,000 on furniture in October 2014.

Nitin's property income for 2014/15 is:

£ ☐

Task 5.5

Sinead starts to let out property on 1 July 2014.

(1) On 1 July 2014, she lets a house which she has owned for several years. The tenant is required to pay annual rent of £8,000, quarterly in advance. The house is let unfurnished. She incurs total allowable expenses of £1,200 in relation to this letting.

(2) On 1 December 2014, she lets out a house which she has bought. The tenant pays annual rent of £450 per month, payable on the first of each month. The house is let unfurnished. She incurs total allowable expenses of £2,000 in relation to this letting.

Sinead's property income for 2014/15 is:

£ ☐

Question bank

Task 5.6

Suzy let out a room in her house at a rent of £500 per month throughout 2014/15. Her allowable expenses for the year were £3,700.

Suzy's property income for 2014/15 is:

£ ⬜

Task 5.7

In 2014/15, Sally makes a property income loss of £(5,000) on letting out Red Roofs, and property income profit of £3,000 on letting out Green Acres. Neither property is qualifying holiday accommodation. Sally also has employment income of £20,000 in 2014/15.

Sally can obtain loss relief by: Tick ONE box

	✓
Setting the loss of £(5,000) against her employment income in 2014/15	
Carrying forward the loss of £(5,000) against property income in 2015/16	
Setting the loss of £(5,000) first against the profit of £3,000 in 2014/15 and then carrying forward the balance of £(2,000) against property income in 2015/16	
Setting the loss of £(5,000) first against the profit of £3,000 in 2014/15 and then setting the balance of £(2,000) against employment income in 2014/15	

Task 5.8

A property can qualify as qualifying holiday accommodation if it is:

Available for letting to the public as holiday accommodation for at least ⬜ days in the tax year and actually let for at least ⬜ days during the same tax year and not normally occupied for periods of 'longer term occupation' (more than 31 consecutive days to the same person) for more than ⬜ days in a tax year.

Question bank

Task 5.9

Tick to show whether the following statement is True or False.

Losses on qualifying holiday accommodation can be set against other income, not just property income.

True	
False	

Task 5.10

Tick to show whether the following statement is True or False.

To be qualifying holiday accommodation, the property must be situated in the UK.

True	
False	

Task 5.11

Olivia let out a room in her house at a rent of £40 per week throughout 2014/15. Her allowable expenses for the year were £2,500.

Olivia's property income loss for 2014/15 is (both brackets and minus signs can be used to indicate negative numbers):

£ [ ]

Task 5.12

Tick to show which ONE of the following is not an advantage of property being qualifying holiday accommodation, as opposed to being taxed under the usual rules for letting furnished property.

	✓
The income qualifies as earnings for pension purposes	
The wear and tear allowance applies	
Capital allowances are available on furniture	

Question bank

Task 5.13

Len owns and lives in a house and he lets out a room to Kathy throughout 2014/15. Kathy pays Len £90 per week. Len estimates that the extra costs of renting the room to Kathy amount to £7 per week.

Tick to show the property income taxable on Len for 2014/15 assuming that he uses the rent a room scheme.

	✓
£90	
£430	
£4,316	
£4,680	

Task 5.14

This style of task is human marked in the live assessment.

Your client Jessica wishes to invest some money which she inherited, by buying accommodation in a popular UK holiday resort. She believes there is a special treatment for income arising from letting out such a property.

Write brief notes explaining the conditions for the special treatment to apply, and the income tax advantages from this treatment.

Task 5.15

Pierce Jones owns a flat that he rents out for £500 per calendar month, payable on the first day of each month. The property is let unfurnished. His other expenses for 2014/15 were:

	£
Electricity and gas	1,200
Water rates	400
Mortgage interest	3,200
Insurance	250

Use this information to complete the Property page, which follows.

Question bank

HM Revenue & Customs

UK property
Tax year 6 April 2014 to 5 April 2015

Your name

Your Unique Taxpayer Reference (UTR)

UK property details

1 Number of properties rented out

2 If all property income ceased in 2014–15 and you do not expect to receive such income in 2015–16, put 'X' in the box and consider if you need to complete the *Capital gains summary* page

3 If you have any income from property let jointly, put 'X' in the box

4 If you are claiming Rent a Room relief and your rents are £4,250 or less nor £2,125 if let jointly), put 'X' in the box

Furnished holiday lettings (FHL) in the UK or European Economic Area (EEA)

Fill in one page for UK businesses and a separate page for EEA businesses. Please read the *UK property notes* before filling in boxes 5 to 19 if you have furnished holiday lettings

5 Income – the amount of rent and any income for services provided to tenants

6 Rent paid, repairs, insurance and costs of services provided – the total amount

7 Loan interest and other financial cost

8 Legal, management and other professional fee

9 Other allowable property expenses

10 Private use adjustment – if expenses include any amounts for non-business purposes

11 Balancing charges – read the notes

12 Capital allowances – read the notes

13 Adjusted profit for the year (if the amount in box 5 + box 10 + box 11 minus (boxes 6 to 9 + box 12) is positive)

14 Loss brought forward used against this year's profit – if you have a non-FHL property business loss read the notes on property losses

15 Taxable profit for the year (box 13 minus box 14)

16 Loss for the year (if the amount in boxes 6 to 9 + box 12 minus (box 5 + box 10 + box 11) is positive)

17 Total loss to carry forward

18 If this business is in the EEA, put 'X' in the box – read the notes

19 If you want to make a period of grace election, put 'X' in the box

SA105 2014   Page UKP 1   HMRC 12/14

Question bank

Property income

Do not include furnished holiday lettings, Real Estate Investment Trust or Property Authorised Investment Funds dividends/distributions here.

20 Total rents and other income from property £ · 0 0	22 Premiums for the grant of a lease – from box E on the Working Sheet – *read the notes* £ · 0 0
21 Tax taken off any income in box 20 £ · 0 0	23 Reverse premiums and inducements £ · 0 0

Property expenses

24 Rent, rates, insurance, ground rents etc £ · 0 0	27 Legal, management and other professional fee £ · 0 0
25 Property repairs, maintenance and renewals £ · 0 0	28 Costs of services provided, including wages £ · 0 0
26 Loan interest and other financial cost £ · 0 0	29 Other allowable property expenses £ · 0 0

Calculating your taxable profit or loss

30 Private use adjustment – *read the notes* £ · 0 0	37 Rent a Room exempt amount £ · 0 0
31 Balancing charges – *read the notes* £ · 0 0	38 Adjusted profit for the year – from box O on the Working Sheet – *read the notes* £ · 0 0
32 Annual Investment Allowance £ · 0 0	39 Loss brought forwa\ 33d used against this year's profit £ · 0 0
33 Business Premises Renovation Allowance (Assisted Areas only) – *read the notes* £ · 0 0	40 Taxable profit for the year (box 38 minus box 39 £ · 0 0
34 All other capital allowances £ · 0 0	41 Adjusted loss for the year – from box O on the Working Sheet – *read the notes* £ · 0 0
35 Landlord's Energy Saving Allowance £ · 0 0	42 Loss set off against 2014–15 total income – *this will be unusual – read the notes* £ · 0 0
36 10% wear and tear allowance – *for furnished residential accommodation only* £ · 0 0	43 Loss to carry forward to following year, including unused losses brought forward £ · 0 0

Sa105 2014   Page UKP 2

Question bank

Payment of tax and tax administration

Task 6.1

Tick to show the correct answer.

By which date should an individual normally submit his 2014/15 self assessment tax return if it is to be filed online?

	✓
31 January 2016	
5 April 2016	
31 October 2015	
31 December 2015	

Task 6.2

Gordon had income tax payable of £14,500 in 2013/14. His income tax payable for 2014/15 was £17,000.

How will Gordon settle his income tax payable for 2014/15?

	✓
The full amount of £17,000 will be paid on 31 January 2016	
Payments on account of £7,250 will be made on 31 January and 31 July 2015, with nothing due on 31 January 2016	
Payments on account of £8,500 will be made on 31 January and 31 July 2015 with nothing due on 31 January 2016	
Payments on account of £7,250 will be made on 31 January and 31 July 2015, with the balance of £2,500 being paid on 31 January 2016	

Question bank

Task 6.3

Pat has property income and dividend income in 2014/15.

What is the latest date until which Pat must retain records of his income?

	✓
All records until 31 January 2017	
Property income until 31 January 2017, dividend income until 31 January 2021	
Property income until 31 January 2021, dividend income until 31 January 2017	
All records until 31 January 2021	

Task 6.4

Tick to show the correct answer.

The minimum penalty as a percentage of Potential Lost Revenue for a deliberate but not concealed error on a tax return, for which is there is an unprompted disclosure is:

	✓
0%	
20%	
30%	
35%	

Task 6.5

The maximum penalty per tax year for failing to keep records is:

£ ☐

Task 6.6

This style of task is human marked in the live assessment.

You have received the following letter from a client:

Dear Peter

Tax advice

I am employed as a general manager for Smith Brothers Ltd, based in Surrey. Up to now I have never had to complete a tax return, but recently I received a return from HMRC for the tax year to 5 April 2015, which I am not sure how to complete. I have arranged, with your secretary, to meet with you on Monday at 11.30 am.

I received and paid the following types of income and expenditure during the last tax year, but I am not sure what information or documents you might require to complete the return.

Income

Salary (£35,000 approximately)

Loan of a company car

Private medical insurance provided by the company

Bank interest

Building society interest

Interest from a New Individual Savings Account

Payments

Contribution to a personal pension plan

Interest on a mortgage on my main residence

Subscription to the Institute of Personnel Managers

I would be grateful if you could inform me as to what I should bring with me to the meeting to help complete the tax return. Also could you answer the following questions?

(a) When must the return be submitted to HMRC?

(b) When will the tax be payable?

(c) Are there any penalties if the deadlines in (a) and (b) are not met; if so what are they?

(d) My wife earns £6,500 a year – does this need to be included on my return?

Yours sincerely
John Hunt

Reply to Mr Hunt's letter.

Question bank

Task 6.7

This style of task is human marked in the live assessment.

You have just submitted the tax return for 2014/15 for your client, Donald Icer, when you receive the following email from him:

From:	Dicer@hotnet.net
To:	AATStudent@boxmail.net
Sent:	30 November 2015
Subject:	Information

I know you have been working on my tax affairs, and I hope you haven't yet submitted the tax return, as I have just realised that there are some things that I haven't told you about.

During 2014/15, I received building society interest of £152 and interest from a NISA of £93. I also paid £100 to the National Trust, under Gift Aid.

I don't know if any of this is important, but I thought I should let you know anyway.

Thanks.

Donald

Reply to Donald's email informing him of:

(a) **The tax implications of each item**
(b) **The consequences of submitting an incorrect tax return**

You are not required to compute the income tax due as a result of these omissions. Donald does not pay income tax at the higher or additional rate.

From:	AATStudent@boxmail.net
To:	Dicer@hotnet.net
Sent:	1 December 2015
Subject:	Information

Task 6.8

This style of task is human marked in the live assessment.

You have just received the following email from your client, Clarissa, whom you have recently started to act for:

From:	clarissa@hotnet.net
To:	AATStudent@boxmail.net
Sent:	15 September 2015
Subject:	Worried

I am worried about my tax return for 2013/14 which I prepared myself. I have just realised that I didn't notify HMRC of interest of £420 on my investment account with National Savings and Investments for that year. I just forgot that I had the account as I rarely deposit or withdraw money from it.

Can you please advise about what I should do and about any penalties or interest that I may incur? I was a basic rate taxpayer in 2013/14.

Thanks.

Clarissa

Reply to Clarissa's email.

From:	AATStudent@boxmail.net
To:	clarissa@hotnet.net
Sent:	17 September 2015
Subject:	Worried

Task 6.9

This style of task is human marked in the live assessment.

June has written to you with the following query:

'I have just had a tax bill from HMRC with the amount that I need to pay on 31 January 2016. You will remember that I started letting out some properties on 1 May 2014. The bill says that I need to pay £5,000 for 2014/15 which is the figure that you told me was my tax liability on my property income for that year. But it also says that I need to pay them £2,500 on 31 January 2016 as well. I don't understand this because my property income will probably be a lot less in 2015/16 than it was in 2014/15.

Please could you explain why I have to pay this extra amount and if there is anything I could do to reduce it.'

Make a list of the points you would make when responding to June's query.

Question bank

Chargeable gains

Task 7.1

For the gain on the disposal of a capital asset to be a chargeable gain there must be a chargeable

> Disposal

of a chargeable

> Asset

by a chargeable

> Person

Task 7.2

Tick to show whether the following assets are chargeable assets or exempt assets for capital gains tax.

Item	Chargeable asset	Exempt asset
Car		✓
A plot of land	✓	
Jewellery	✓	
Premium bonds		✓
Government stock ('gilts')		✓

Question bank

Task 7.3

Tick to show which ONE of the following is not a chargeable disposal for capital gains purposes.

	✓
The gift of an asset	
The sale of part of an asset	
The transfer of an asset on death	✓
The sale of the whole of an asset	

Task 7.4

Kate purchased a freehold property for £40,000. Kate then spent £5,000 on a new roof for the property as the old roof was storm damaged prior to acquisition. She sold the property for £90,000 on 15 March 2015. Kate had not made any other disposals during 2014/15.

What is Kate's taxable gain for 2014/15?

	✓
£34,000	✓
£39,000	
£45,000	✗
£50,000	

90000
(45000)
45000
(11000)
34000

40000
5000
45000

Task 7.5

In November 2014, Lenny made chargeable gains of £20,000 and allowable losses of £3,560. He made no other disposals during 2014/15 and is a higher rate taxpayer.

(1) **Lenny's capital gains tax liability for 2014/15 is:**

£ 1523.20   1523

(2) **Lenny's capital gains tax liability is payable by:** (insert date as xx/xx/xxxx)

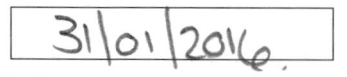

31/01/2016

Question bank

Task 7.6

In November 2014, Larry made chargeable gains of £25,000 and allowable losses of £5,200. He made no other disposals during 2014/15. He has £4,000 of his basic rate tax band remaining.

Larry's capital gains tax liability for 2014/15 is:

£ ☐

Task 7.7

Laura made chargeable gains of £5,000 in July 2014 and £17,500 in November 2014. In May 2014 she made allowable losses of £2,000. Laura has taxable income of £29,800 for 2014/15.

Laura's capital gains tax liability for 2014/15 is:

£ ☐

Task 7.8

Lisa made chargeable gains of £27,000 in December 2014. She made no other disposals in the year. Her taxable income for 2014/15 was £25,900.

Lisa's capital gains tax liability for 2014/15 is:

£ ☐

Task 7.9

Darren bought a 3 acre plot of land for £150,000. He sold two acres of the land at auction for £240,000. His disposal costs were £3,000. The market value of the one remaining acre at the date of sale was £60,000.

(1) **The cost of the land sold is:**

£ 120000

(2) **The chargeable gain on sale is:**

£ 117000

Question bank

Task 7.10

Tick to show how a taxpayer will pay the capital gains tax due for 2014/15.

	✓
The full amount will be paid on 31 January 2016	
The full amount will be paid on 31 January 2015	
Payments on account will be made on 31 January and 31 July 2015, with the balance being paid on 31 January 2016	
Payments on account will be made on 31 January and 31 July 2014, with the balance being paid on 31 January 2015	

Task 7.11

Mattheus made gains of £18,200 and losses of £7,000 in 2014/15. He has losses brought forward of £5,000.

The losses to carry forward to 2015/16 are (do not use brackets or a minus sign):

£ [   ]

Task 7.12

Mike inherited a valuable painting from a distant uncle in November 2006. The painting was valued at £9,000 at the date of the uncle's death. Luckily for Mike, when he sold it in December 2014, the proceeds were £16,000.

Mike's chargeable gain on sale is:

£ [   ]

Task 7.13

Luke sells one acre of land in August 2014 for £25,000. His disposal costs were £2,500. He had bought four acres of land for £15,000. The market value of the remaining land was £50,000 at the date of sale. The acquisition costs of the four acres of land were £1,500.

Luke's chargeable gain on sale is:

£ 17,000

Question bank

Task 7.14

Tick to show whether the following statement is True or False.

If an individual has allowable losses brought forward, these are only used to bring gains down to the annual exempt amount.

	✓
True	
False	

Task 7.15

James has the following gains and losses arising from disposals of chargeable assets:

Tax year	2012/13	2013/14	2014/15
Gains	£2,000	£4,000	£13,400
Losses	£(14,000)	£(2,000)	£(2,000)

The maximum allowable loss carried forward to 2015/16 will be:

£ ☐

Task 7.16

Mary is married to Mike. Mike has a sister, Susan who is married to Simon. Susan and Simon have a daughter called Sarah.

Tick which ONE of the following is not a connected person in relation to Mary.

	✓
Mike	
Susan	
Simon	
Sarah	✓

Question bank

Task 7.17

Joanne gives an asset to her son in September 2014. There was an allowable loss on the disposal of £(3,000). Joanne also gave an asset to her daughter in October 2014. There was a chargeable gain of £5,000 on this disposal.

Tick to show whether the following statement is True or False.

The loss of £(3,000) can be set against the gain of £5,000.

	✓
True	
False	

Task 7.18

Xena bought a vase for £1,500 and sold it in October 2014 for £6,500, incurring expenses of sale of £130.

Her chargeable gain on sale is:

£ 833⅓

Task 7.19

Jolyon purchased a gold ring for £7,000. He sold it in January 2015 for £3,000. The expenses of sale were £125.

Jolyon's allowable loss is (do not use brackets or a minus sign):

£ 1125

Task 7.20

Rowenna bought a necklace for £4,000. She sold it in September 2014 for £5,500.

Tick to show whether the following statement is True or False.

Rowenna has a chargeable gain on sale of £1,500.

	✓
True	
False	✓

Task 7.21

Gilda purchased a picture for £3,500 and sold it in September 2014 for £7,500, incurring £300 expenses of sale.

Tick to show the chargeable gain on sale of the picture.

£1,200	
£2,000	
£2,500	✓
£3,700	

Task 7.22

Mark purchased an antique vase for £9,000. He sold the vase in August 2014 at auction for £4,500 net of auctioneer's fees of £500.

Mark's allowable loss is (both minus signs and brackets can be used to indicate negative numbers):

£ (3500)

Task 7.23

Your client, Isabel Redding, has given you the following information about her capital gains position for 2014/15:

Asset sold	Proceeds	Cost
Listed shares in Vodafone plc	£7,000	£9,500
Unlisted shares in Willard Ltd	£5,000	£2,800
Plot of land	£30,000	£13,100

She also has losses of £(1,750) brought forward from 2013/14.

Using this information, complete the capital gains tax summary on the next two pages.

Question bank

Capital gains summary
Tax year 6 April 2014 to 5 April 2015

HM Revenue & Customs

1	Your name

2	Your Unique Taxpayer Reference (UTR)

Summary of your enclosed computations

Please read the *Capital gains summary notes* before filling in this section. **You must enclose your computations, including details of each gain or loss, as well as filling in the boxes.**

To get notes and helpsheets that will help you fill in this form, go to hmrc.gov.uk/selfassessmentforms

3 Total gains *(Boxes 21 + 27 + 33 + 34)*
£ · 0 0

4 Gains qualifying for Entrepreneurs' Relief (but excluding gains deferred from before 23 June 2010) - *read the notes*
£ · 0 0

5 Gains invested under Seed Enterprise Investment Scheme and qualifying for exemption - *read the notes*
£ · 0 0

6 Total losses of the year - *enter '0' if there are none*
£ · 0 0

7 Losses brought forward and used in the year
£ · 0 0

8 Adjustment to Capital Gains Tax - *read the notes*
£ · 0 0

9 Additional liability for non-resident or dual resident trusts
£ · 0 0

10 Losses available to be carried forward to later years
£ · 0 0

11 Losses used against an earlier year's gain (special circumstances apply - *read the notes*)
£ · 0 0

12 Losses used against income - amount claimed against 2014-15 income - *read the notes*
£ · 0 0

13 Amount in box 12 relating to shares to which Enterprise Investment Scheme/Seed Enterprise Investment Scheme relief is attributable
£ · 0 0

14 Losses used against income - amount claimed against 2013-14 income - *read the notes*
£ · 0 0

15 Amount in box 14 relating to shares to which Enterprise Investment Scheme/Seed Enterprise Investment Scheme relief is attributable
£ · 0 0

16 Income losses of 2014-15 set against gains
£ · 0 0

17 Deferred gains from before 23 June 2010 qualifying for Entrepreneurs' Relief
£ · 0 0

SA108 2014   Page CG 1   HMRC 12/14

Listed shares and securities

18 Number of disposals - *read the notes*

19 Disposal proceeds
£

20 Allowable costs (including purchase price)
£

21 Gains in the year, before losses
£

22 If you are making any claim or election, put 'X' in the box

23 If your computations include any estimates or valuations, put 'X' in the box

Unlisted shares and securities

24 Number of disposals - *read the notes*

25 Disposal proceeds
£

26 Allowable costs (including purchase price)
£

27 Gains in the year, before losses
£

28 If you are making any claim or election, put 'X' in the box

29 If your computations include any estimates or valuations, put 'X' in the box

Property and other assets and gains

30 Number of disposals

31 Disposal proceeds
£

32 Allowable costs (including purchase price)
£

33 Gains in the year, before losses
£

34 Attributed gains where personal losses cannot be set off
£

35 If you are making any claim or election, put 'X' in the box

36 If your computations include any estimates or valuations, put 'X' in the box

Any other information

37 Please give any other information in this space

SA108 2014   Page CG 2

Question bank

Share disposals

Task 8.1

Mr Stevens sold 5,000 ordinary shares for £20,000 in JKL plc on 10 August 2014. He bought 6,000 shares in JKL plc for £9,000 on 15 July 2013 and another 1,000 shares for £4,200 on 16 August 2014.

His net chargeable gain on sale is:

£ [   ]

Task 8.2

On 17 January 2015 Lionel sold 10,000 ordinary shares in Old plc. He had originally purchased 12,000 shares in Old plc on 10 May 2007, and purchased another 8,000 shares on 24 January 2015.

Tick to show how Lionel's disposal of 10,000 shares in Old plc will be matched with his acquisitions.

	✓
Against 10,000 of the shares purchased on 10 May 2007	
Against 5,000 of the shares purchased on 24 January 2015 and then against 5,000 of the shares purchased on 10 May 2007	
Against 10,000 of the total shareholding of 20,000 shares	
Against the 8,000 shares purchased on 24 January 2015 and then against 2,000 of the shares purchased on 10 May 2007	

Question bank

Task 8.3

This style of task is human marked in the live assessment.

Eloise's dealings in Moo plc were as follows:

	No. of shares	Cost/(proceeds)
		£
10 February 2000	12,000	18,000
20 September 2007	Bonus issue of 1 for 4	Nil
15 March 2015	(2,000)	(8,000)

Using the proforma layout provided, calculate Eloise's gain on sale. Fill in all the unshaded boxes and if the answer is zero insert '0'. Both minus signs and brackets can be used to indicate negative numbers.

Share pool

	No. of shares	Cost £
10 February 2000		
20 September 2007 Bonus 1:4		
15 March 2015 Disposal		

Gain on sale

	£
Proceeds	
Less cost	
Gain	

Question bank

Task 8.4

This style of task is human marked in the live assessment.

Mark sold 10,000 of his shares in AC plc on 4 November 2014 for £60,000. The shares had been acquired as follows:

	No. of shares	Cost £
9 December 2000	12,000	4,400
12 October 2004 (rights issue 1:3 at £5)		
10 November 2014	2,000	11,500

Calculate Mark's total chargeable gain on sale. All workings must be shown. If the answer is zero insert '0'. Both minus signs and brackets can be used to indicate negative numbers.

Question bank

Principal private residence

Task 9.1

Nicole is selling her main residence, which she has owned for 25 years. She lived in the house for the first 8 years of ownership, let the property for the next 5 years whilst she was posted abroad by her employer, returned to live in the house for the next 2 years, and then moved out for the remainder of her period of ownership.

Tick to show what fraction of her gain will be exempt under the private residence exemption.

	✓
16.5/25	
8.5/25	
15.5/25	
11.5/25	

Task 9.2

Mr Fox bought a house on 1 August 1996 for £50,000. He lived in the house until 31 July 1999. He then went abroad to work as a self-employed engineer until 31 July 2004. He lived in the house again until 31 January 2005, when he moved out.

Mr Fox sold the house on 31 July 2014 for £180,000.

Using the proforma layout provided, calculate the chargeable gain on sale.

	£
Proceeds	
Less cost	
Gain before PPR exemption	
Less PPR exemption	
Chargeable gain	

Question bank

Answer bank

Answer bank

The tax framework

Task 1.1

The tax year 2014/15 runs from:

| 06/04/2014 |

until

| 05/04/2015 |

Task 1.2

Detailed regulations relating to tax law are contained in Statutory Instruments.

	✓
True	✓
False	

Task 1.3

The UK tax system is administered by:

	✓
Parliament	
Her Majesty's Revenue & Customs (HMRC)	✓
Serious Organised Crime Agency (SOCA)	
HM Customs & Excise	

Task 1.4

If you are employed by a firm of accountants, and suspect that one of your clients may be engaged in money laundering, whom should you inform about your suspicions?

	✓
HMRC	
Your firm's Money Laundering Reporting Officer	✓
Serious Organised Crime Agency	
Tax Tribunal	

Task 1.5

Please be assured that an ethical guideline of confidentiality applies in your dealings with our firm.

This guideline means that your personal information will remain confidential, unless you give us authority to disclose information to third parties such as members of your family.

Task 1.6

An accountant is able to disclose information about a client without their permission in TWO of the following situations.

	✓
If the client is unwell and unable to respond to HMRC	
If money laundering is suspected	✓
Where it would be illegal not to disclose the information	✓
If the information is requested from a 'connected person'	

Answer bank

Task 1.7

The five fundamental principles on professional ethics for AAT members are:

I	Integrity
O	Objectivity
Pc and dc	Professional competence and due care
C	Confidentiality
Pb	Professional behaviour

Task 1.8

If you are a sole practitioner, and suspect that one of your clients may be engaged in money laundering, whom should you inform about your suspicions?

	✓
HMRC	
Another firm's Money Laundering Reporting Officer	
Serious Organised Crime Agency	✓
Tax Tribunal	

Answer bank

Taxable income

Task 2.1

	Non-savings income	Savings income	Dividend income
Trading income	✓		
Dividend received from a company			✓
Property income	✓		
Building society interest		✓	
Bank interest		✓	
Pension income	✓		
Employment income	✓		
Interest from government stock ('gilts')		✓	

Task 2.2

(a) Bank account interest £160

£ | 200

£160 × 100/80

(b) Premium bond prize £100

£ | 0

Premium bond prizes are exempt income

(c) Dividends received £540

£ | 600

£540 × 100/90

Answer bank

Task 2.3

The age allowance Bob is entitled to for 2014/15 is:

£	10,100

	£
Age allowance (born between 6/4/1938 and 5/4/1948)	10,500
Less ½ × £(27,800 – 27,000)	(400)
Age allowance	10,100

Task 2.4

	Gross	Net	Exempt
Interest on NS&I savings certificate			✓
Bank interest		✓	
Interest on NS&I investment account	✓		
Interest on (new) individual savings account			✓
Interest on NS&I Direct Saver account	✓		
Building society interest		✓	
Interest from government stock ('gilts')	✓		

Answer bank

Task 2.5

Jonty's taxable income for 2014/15 is:

£ 28,300

	Non-savings income £	Savings income £	Dividend income £	Total £
Earnings	38,130			
Building society interest (£80 × 100/80)		100		
Dividends (£63 × 100/90)			70	
Net income	38,130	100	70	38,300
Less personal allowance	(10,000)			(10,000)
Taxable income	28,130	100	70	28,300

Task 2.6

	Non-savings income £	Savings income £	Total £
Earnings	15,065	0	
Bank deposit interest (£457 × 100/80)	0	571	
Building society interest (£400 × 100/80)	0	500	
NISA interest: exempt	0	0	
Net income	15,065	1,071	16,136
Less personal allowance	(10,000)	0	(10,000)
Taxable income	5,065	1,071	6,136

Answer bank

Task 2.7

(1) Hayley's net income for 2014/15 is:

£ 102,000

	Non-savings income £	Savings income £	Dividend income £	Total £
Employment income	95,000			
Bank interest (£1,600 × 100/80)		2,000		
Dividends (£4,500 × 100/90)			5,000	
Net income	95,000	2,000	5,000	102,000

(2) The personal allowance that Hayley is entitled to for 2014/15 is:

£ 9,000

	£
Net income	102,000
Less income limit	(100,000)
Excess	2,000
Personal allowance	10,000
Less half excess	(1,000)
	9,000

76

Task 2.8

Max's personal allowance for 2014/15 is:

£ 4,500

	£
Net income	115,000
Less: Gift Aid donations (gross)	(4,000)
Adjusted net income	111,000
Less income limit	(100,000)
Excess	11,000
Personal allowance	10,000
Less half excess	(5,500)
	4,500

Task 2.9

(1) Gavin's net income for 2014/15 is:

£ 27,500

	Non-savings income £	Savings income £	Dividend income £	Total £
Pension income	19,000			
Bank interest (£2,000 × 100/80)		2,500		
Dividends (£5,400 × 100/90)			6,000	
Net income	19,000	2,500	6,000	27,500

Answer bank

(2) The age allowance that Gavin is entitled to for 2014/15 is:

£ | 10,410

	£
Net income	27,500
Less income limit	(27,000)
Excess	500
Age allowance (born before 6/4/1938)	10,660
Less half excess	(250)
	10,410

Task 2.10

(1) Sue's net income for 2014/15 is:

£ | 27,750

	Non-savings income	Savings income	Dividend income	Total
	£	£	£	£
Pension income	17,000			
Bank interest (£3,000 × 100/80)		3,750		
Dividends (£6,300 × 100/90)			7,000	
Net income	17,000	3,750	7,000	27,750

(2) The age allowance that Sue is entitled to for 2014/15 is:

£ 10,285

	£
Net income	27,750
Less income limit	(27,000)
Excess	750
Age allowance (born before 6/4/1938)	10,660
Less half excess	(375)
	10,285

Task 2.11

The age allowance that Ron is entitled to for 2014/15 is:

£ 10,000

	£
Net income	33,000
Less Gift Aid donation (gross)	(1,500)
Adjusted net income	31,500
Less income limit	(27,000)
Excess	4,500
Age allowance	10,500
Less half excess	(2,250)
	8,250
Minimum allowance	10,000

Answer bank

Task 2.12

From 1 July 2014 the maximum an individual can invest for the tax year in an NISA is:

£	15,000

Task 2.13

Scholarships and educational grants are exempt as income of the student.

	✓
True	✓
False	

Task 2.14

The statement is false. Damages received for both injury and death are always exempt from income tax.

	✓
True	
False	✓

Answer bank

Calculation of income tax

Task 3.1

(1) Guy's income tax liability on the bank interest is:

£ | 1,687

	Non-savings income	Savings income	Total
	£	£	£
Bank interest (£7,500 × 100/80)		9,375	
Taxable income (net of PA)	1,000	9,375	10,375

Tax on bank interest only:

£2,880 – £1,000 = £1,880 × 10%	188
£9,375 – £1,880 = £7,495 × 20%	1,499
Income tax liability	1,687

(2) Guy's income tax liability on the bank interest is:

£ | 3,377

	Non-savings income	Savings income	Total
	£	£	£
Bank interest (£7,500 × 100/80)		9,375	
Taxable income (net of PA)	30,000	9,375	39,375

Tax on bank interest only:

£31,865 – £30,000 = £1,865 × 20%	373
£9,375 – £1,865 = £7,510 × 40%	3,004
Income tax liability	3,377

Answer bank

Task 3.2

(1) The tax credit attached to this dividend is:

| £ | 657 |

£5,913 net dividend × 100/90 = £6,570 gross dividend

Tax credit is £6,570 × 10% = £657

Alternatively a quicker way to calculate the tax credit is to multiply the net dividend received by 10/90 which gives £5,913 × 10/90 = £657

(2) The rate of tax Holly will pay on this dividend (ignoring the effect of the tax credit) is:

| 32.5 | % |

Task 3.3

(1) Non-savings income:

| £ | 2,940 |

(2) Savings income:

| £ | 435 |

(3) Dividend income:

| £ | 177 |

	Non-savings income £	Savings income £	Dividend income £	Total £
Taxable income	14,700	2,176	1,766	18,642
Tax on non-savings income:	£14,700 × 20%		2,940	
Tax on savings income:	£2,176 × 20%		435	
Tax on dividend income:	£1,766 × 10%		177	
Income tax liability			3,552	

Answer bank

Task 3.4

	✓
£37,865	
£31,865	
£39,365	✓
£36,665	

Basic rate band extended by the gross Gift Aid donation, ie £(6,000 × 100/80) = £7,500

£31,865 + £7,500 = £39,365

Task 3.5

(1) Katy's basic rate band for 2014/15 is:

£	36,865

Basic rate band extended by the gross Gift Aid donation, ie £(4,000 × 100/80) = £5,000

£31,865 + £5,000

(2) Katy's higher rate band for 2014/15 is:

£	118,135

(3) Katy's additional rate threshold for 2014/15 is:

£	155,000

Additional rate threshold = £36,865 + £118,135 (or £150,000 + £5,000)

Answer bank

Task 3.6

Rachel's income tax liability for 2014/15 is:

£ 712

	£
Net income £12,000 × 100/80	15,000
Less personal allowance	(10,000)
Taxable income	5,000
£2,880 @ 10%	288
£5,000 – 2,880 = £2,120 × 20%	424
Income tax liability	712

Task 3.7

Richard's income tax payable for 2014/15 is:

£ 4,637

		Non-savings income
		£
Taxable income		58,525

	£		£
Tax	31,865 × 20%		6,373
	13,500 (extended by £10,800 x 100/80) @ 20%		2,700
	45,365		
	13,160 × 40%		5,264
	58,525		
Income tax liability			14,337
Less tax suffered at source (PAYE)			(9,700)
Income tax payable			4,637

Task 3.8

(1)

	Non-savings income	Savings income	Dividend income	Total
	£	£	£	£
Salary	50,000	0	0	
Dividend £900 × 100/90	0	0	1,000	
Bank deposit interest £800 × 100/80	0	1,000	0	
Net income	50,000	1,000	1,000	52,000
Less personal allowance	(10,000)	0	0	(10,000)
Taxable income	40,000	1,000	1,000	42,000

(2) John's income tax liability for 2014/15 is:

£ 9,752

(3) John's income tax payable for 2014/15 is:

£ 952

	£
Tax on non-savings income	
£31,865 × 20%	6,373
£3,000 (extended band: Gift Aid £2,400 × 100/80) × 20%	600
£5,135 (£40,000 – 31,865 – 3,000) × 40%	2,054
Tax on savings income	
£1,000 × 40%	400
Tax on dividend income	
£1,000 × 32.5%	325
Income tax liability	9,752
Less tax credit on dividend income (£1,000 × 10%)	(100)
Less tax suffered on bank interest (£1,000 × 20%)	(200)
Less PAYE (given)	(8,500)
Income tax payable	952

Answer bank

Task 3.9

(1)

	Non-savings income	Savings income	Dividend income	Total
	£	£	£	£
Salary	155,000	0	0	
Dividend £4,500 × 100/90	0	0	5,000	
Bank deposit interest £2,400 × 100/80	0	3,000	0	
Net income	155,000	3,000	5,000	163,000
Less personal allowance	0	0	0	0
Taxable income	155,000	3,000	5,000	163,000

The net income is in excess of £120,000 so the personal allowance is reduced to nil.

(2) Jean's income tax liability for 2014/15 is:

£ 56,602

(3) Jean's income tax payable for 2014/15 is:

£ 7,002

	£
Tax on non-savings income	
£31,865 × 20%	6,373
£10,000 (extended band: pension) £8,000 × 100/80 × 20%	2,000
£113,135 × 40%	45,254
Tax on savings income	
£3,000 × 40%	1,200
Tax on dividend income	
£2,000 × 32.5%	650
£3,000 × 37.5%	1,125
Income tax liability	56,602

Answer bank

Income tax liability b/fwd		56,602
Less tax deducted at source		
tax credit on dividend income (£5,000 × 10%)		(500)
tax suffered on bank interest (£3,000 × 20%)		(600)
PAYE (given)		(48,500)
Income tax payable		7,002

Note: Additional rate threshold is increased by £10,000 to £160,000. Therefore only £3,000 of the dividend income is taxed at the additional rate.

Task 3.10

	Non-savings income £	Savings income £	Dividend income £	Total £
Pension income	9,200			
Bank interest £4,300 × 100/80		5,375		
Dividends £13,500 × 100/90			15,000	
Net income	9,200	5,375	15,000	29,575
Personal allowance (W)	(9,200)	(950)		(10,150)
Taxable income	Nil	4,425	15,000	19,425
Tax on savings income:				
£2,880 × 10%		288		
£1,545 (£4,425 – £2,880) × 20%		309		
Tax on dividend income:				
£15,000 × 10%		1,500		
Income tax liability		2,097		

Answer bank

Working

	£
Net income	29,575
Less Gift Aid donation (£1,500 × 100/80)	(1,875)
Adjusted net income	27,700
Less income limit	(27,000)
Excess	700
Age allowance	10,500
Less half excess	(350)
Adjusted age allowance	10,150

Task 3.11

Amanda's age allowance for 2014/15 is:

£ 10,375

	Non-savings income	Dividend income	Total
	£	£	£
Pension income	24,000		
Dividend income (£3,555 × 100/90)		3,950	
Net income	24,000	3,950	27,950

	£
Net income	27,950
Less Gift Aid donation (£304 × 100/80)	(380)
Adjusted net income	27,570
Less income limit	(27,000)
Excess	570
Age allowance	10,660
Less half excess (570 × ½)	(285)
Adjusted age allowance	10,375

Answer bank

Answer bank

Employment income

Task 4.1

	✓
True	
False	✓

An employee has a contract of service.

Task 4.2

Factor	Contract of service	Contract for services
Peter is entitled to paid holidays	✓	
Peter hires his own helpers		✓
Peter takes substantial financial risks when undertaking work for XYZ plc		✓
Peter does not have to rectify mistakes in his work at his own expense	✓	

Task 4.3

Item	£
Salary	24,280
Commission	0
Employer's pension contribution	0
Bonus	1,200

Salary paid on the first of each month, therefore received in 2014/15 as follows:

1 May 2014 to 1 September 2014 = 5 × £2,000 = £10,000

1 October 2014 to 1 April 2015 = 7 × £2,000 × 102% = £14,280

Salary = £10,000 + £14,280 = £24,280

Answer bank

Task 4.4

True	
False	✓

Tips received by a tour guide from customers are earnings. Note that earnings can include money received other than from the employer.

Task 4.5

The date of receipt of the bonus for employment income purposes is:

| 20/12/2014 |

Task 4.6

(1) The cost of the car in the taxable benefit computation is:

| £ | 15,000 |

(2) The percentage used in the taxable benefit computation is:

| 32 | % |

The CO_2 emissions of the car are 195g/km (rounded down to the nearest five).

Amount over baseline figure: 195 – 95 = 100g/km

Divide 100 by 5 = 20

The taxable percentage is 12% + 20% = 32%

(3) The taxable benefit on the provision of the car is:

| £ | 3,200 |

32% × £15,000 × 8/12 (6 August 2014 to 5 April 2015)

Answer bank

Task 4.7

(1) The taxable benefit on the provision of the car is:

£ | 5,900

Round down CO_2 emissions to 170 g/km

Amount above baseline: 170 – 95 = 75 g/km

Divide 75 by 5 = 15

Taxable % = 12% + 15% + 3% (diesel) = 30%

	£
£25,000 × 30% × 10/12	6,250
Less employee contribution (10 × £35)	(350)
Taxable benefit of car	5,900

(2) The taxable benefit on the provision of fuel is:

£ | 5,425

£21,700 × 30% × 10/12 = £5,425

Task 4.8

(1) The cost of the car in the taxable benefit computation is:

£ | 11,500

(2) The percentage used in the taxable benefit computation is:

8 | %

As CO_2 emissions are 75g/km or less = 5% + 3% (diesel)

(3) The taxable benefit in respect of the provision of fuel for private use is:

£ | 1,736

£21,700 × 8%

Answer bank

Task 4.9

(1) The percentage used in the taxable benefit computation is:

25	
35	✓
37	
34	

Round down CO_2 emissions to 205 g/km

Amount above baseline: 205 – 95 = 110 g/km

Divide 110 by 5 = 22

Taxable % = 12% + 22% + 3% (diesel) = 37%, max 35%

(2) The taxable benefit in respect of the provision of the car is:

£ 18,200

	£
List price	57,000
Less capital contribution paid by employee (max)	(5,000)
Cost of car	52,000
Car benefit @ 35%	18,200

(3) The taxable benefit in respect of the provision of fuel for private use is:

£ 7,595

£21,700 × 35% = £7,595 There is no reduction for part reimbursement of private fuel.

Task 4.10

	✓
£3,090	
£3,671	
£3,590	
nil	✓

There is no taxable benefit because there is no private use of the van – travel from home to work is not private use for vans.

Task 4.11

The taxable benefit for 2014/15 is:

£ | 110

The benefit taxable in 2013/14 was 20% × £200 = £40

The benefit taxable in 2014/15 will be the greater of:

		£	£
(a)	Market value at acquisition by employee	120	
(b)	Original market value	200	
	Less benefit for use in 2013/14	(40)	
		160	
	ie		160
	Less price paid by employee		(50)
	Taxable benefit 2014/15		110

Answer bank

Task 4.12

(1) Using the average method, the taxable benefit for 2014/15 is:

£ | 138

	£
3.25% × (50,000 + 20,000)/2	1,138
Less interest paid	(1,000)
Taxable benefit	138

(2) Using the alternative method, the taxable benefit for 2014/15 is:

£ | 300

	£
£50,000 × 8/12 × 3.25%	1,083
(6 April 2014 to 5 December 2014)	
£20,000 × 4/12 × 3.25%	217
(6 December 2014 to 5 April 2015)	
	1,300
Less interest paid	(1,000)
Taxable benefit	300

Task 4.13

	✓
True	
False	✓

There is a taxable benefit of the amount of the loan written-off, however small the loan. The £10,000 limit only applies to the interest benefit.

Task 4.14

(1) The taxable benefit for 2014/15 is:

£ 650

During 2014/15 Vimal will have a taxable benefit arising from the use of the asset:

£1,000 × 20% × 9/12 = £150

He will also have a benefit when the asset is sold to him at an undervalue.

This will be the higher of the MV at the date of the 'gift', and the original market value minus benefits assessed so far, less his £100 contribution.

	£	£
Market value at date of gift		300
Original market value		1,000
Assessed re use:		
2012/13 £1,000 × 20% × 3/12	50	
2013/14 £1,000 × 20%	200	
2014/15 £1,000 × 20% × 9/12	150	
		(400)
		600
ie Higher value used		600
Less Vimal's contribution		(100)
		500
His total benefit (for both use and 'gift') in 2014/15 will therefore be		650

(2) The taxable benefit for 2014/15 is:

£ 4,463

The taxable benefit for use of the flat is calculated as follows:

	£
Annual value	3,000
£(120,000 – 75,000) × 3.25% (expensive accommodation)	1,463
Taxable benefit	4,463

The original cost is used, not the value now.

Answer bank

Task 4.15

The total taxable benefits for 2014/15 are:

£ 625

	£
Medical insurance (cost to employer)	385
Childcare (exempt – £55 per week for a basic rate taxpayer)	0
Newspaper allowance (12 × £20)	240
Taxable benefits	625

Task 4.16

(1) The taxable benefit arising in respect of the accommodation provided for Rita in 2014/15 and purchase of the furniture is:

£ 21,200

	£
Annual value (higher than rent paid)	4,000
Electricity	700
Gas	1,200
Water	500
Council tax	1,300
Repairs	3,500
Furniture (20% × £30,000 × 6/12)	3,000
Purchase of furniture (W)	7,000
	21,200

Working

Purchase of furniture

Benefit is the **higher** of:

			£
(a)	Cost		30,000
	Less taxed for use of furniture (20% × £30,000 × 6/12)		(3,000)
			27,000
	Less amount paid by Rita		(20,000)
			7,000
(b)	Market value		25,000
	Less amount paid		(20,000)
			5,000

(2) The taxable benefit arising in respect of the relocation expenses is:

£ 4,000

£12,000 – £8,000

(3) The taxable benefit arising in respect of the interest free loan in 2014/15 is:

£ 325

£10,000 × 3.25%

Answer bank

Task 4.17

	✓
£800	
£1,515	
£315	✓
£715	

	£
Annual value	800
Less contribution (£100 × 12 = £1,200)	(800)
	NIL

Additional charge

	£	£
Cost	97,000	
Less	(75,000)	
Excess	22,000	
£22,000 × 3.25%		715
Less contribution (£1,200 – £800)		(400)
Total benefit 2014/15		315

Task 4.18

	✓
Taxable benefit of £700	
Allowable expense of £700	✓
Allowable expense of £1,300	
Taxable benefit of £4,550	

	£	£
Amount received 13,000 × 35p		4,550
Less statutory amounts		
10,000 × 45p	4,500	
3,000 × 25p	750	
		(5,250)
Allowable expense		(700)

Answer bank

Task 4.19

Item	Taxable	Exempt
Interest on loan of £2,000 (only loan provided)		✓
Removal costs of £6,000		✓
Use of pool car		✓
Reimbursement of business expenses under a dispensation		✓
One staff party costing £100 per head		✓
Accommodation provided to employee who is not required to live in it for the performance of employment	✓	
Provision of parking space at work		✓
Additional costs of home-working of £4 per week		✓
Long service award of £800 for 22 years service		✓
Accommodation provided to a caretaker for proper performance of his employment duties		✓
Work related training		✓
Provision of second mobile phone	✓	

Task 4.20

	£
Salary	30,000
Less allowable expenses:	
reimbursed expenses	0
pension contribution (£30,000 × 8%)	(2,400)
professional body membership	(150)
fitness club membership	0
charitable donation (£50 × 12)	(600)
clothing	0
Employment income 2014/15	26,850

Answer bank

Task 4.21

The maximum amount of relocation expenses that his employer can pay without a taxable benefit arising is:

£ 8,000

Task 4.22

	✓
£3,600	
£20,000	✓
£26,300	
£27,000	

The maximum contribution is the higher of £3,600 and his earnings of £20,000.

Dividends are not earnings.

Task 4.23

Zara's qualifying travel expenses for 2014/15 are:

£ 2,100

£300 + £1,800. Travel expenses from home to a permanent workplace are not allowable.

Task 4.24

	✓
The employer deducts the contribution after calculating income tax under PAYE.	
The employer deducts basic rate tax from the contribution and the employee gets higher rate relief by extending the basic rate band in the tax computation.	
The employer deducts the contribution before calculating income tax under PAYE.	✓
The employer deducts basic rate tax from the contribution and there is no higher rate tax relief.	

The employer deducts the contribution before calculating income tax, so giving tax relief at the applicable rate/s.

Answer bank

Task 4.25

	✓
The pension contribution is paid net of basic rate tax, and higher rate tax relief is obtained by extending the basic rate band.	
The contribution is deducted from employment income as an allowable expense before tax is calculated under PAYE.	✓

Task 4.26

From:	AATStudent@boxmail.net
To:	MartinWilkes@boxmail.net
Sent:	14 March 2015 12:29
Subject:	Car

The car benefit is a percentage of the car's list price, not the actual price paid by the employer.

The percentage (that is multiplied by the list price) is dependant on the car's CO_2 emissions rating. For cars which emit CO_2 of 95g/km or more the percentage is 12%, however this percentage increases by 1% for every additional whole 5g/km of CO_2 emissions above 95g/km, up to a maximum of 35%.

In this case, the percentage would be 12% + 15% = 27%.

The percentage is further increased by 3% for a diesel car – has this car got a petrol or a diesel engine?

As the employer will be paying for fuel used for private motoring, a fuel benefit arises. The benefit is a percentage of £21,700. The percentage is the same percentage as is used to calculate the car benefit.

No benefit arises if you reimburse the whole of the expense of any fuel provided for private use, but there is **no** reduction to the benefit if only part of the expense for private use fuel is reimbursed, as here. It would be better for the contribution to be set against the use of the car, as this would be deductible in calculating the car benefit.

Task 4.27

Name	Jill Gilks
Box 1	60000.00
Box 2	13900.00
Box 5	Beata plc
Box 9	5200.00
Box 10	2000.00
Box 16	2250.00
Box 17	2250.00
Box 19	225.00

Answer bank

Property income

Task 5.1

Simran's property income for 2014/15 is:

£2,080	
£1,990	
£2,040	
£2,130	✓

	£
Rent received (9 months × £500 – accruals basis)	4,500
Less electricity	(1,200)
water rates	(500)
insurance 9/12 × £360	(270)
wear and tear £(4,500 – 500) × 10%	(400)
Property income 2014/15	2,130

Task 5.2

What amount of taxable property income does Julie have for 2014/15?

£ 3,120

	£
Rent received (£6,300 × 8/12)	4,200
Less expenses:	(660)
wear and tear (£4,200 × 10%)	(420)
Property income 2014/15	3,120

Room in own house

Exempt under rent a room (gross rent less than £4,250)

Answer bank

Task 5.3

Zelda's property income for 2014/15 is:

| £ | 4,500 |

2012/13
£(6,000 – 10,000) = £(4,000)

2013/14
£(8,000 – 5,500) = £2,500
less use loss b/f £(2,500)
Nil

2014/15
£(10,000 – 4,000) = £6,000
less use rest of loss £(1,500)

Taxable property income 2014/15 £4,500

Task 5.4

Nitin's property income for 2014/15 is:

| £ | 4,154 |

	£
Rent (£3,600 × 3)	10,800
Rent (£4,000 × 1)	4,000
	14,800
Less water rates	(195)
insurance (£440 × 6/11)	(240)
interest (£350,000 × 5% × 6/12)	(8,750)
initial repairs: capital	0
Wear and tear allowance £(14,800 – 195) × 10%	(1,461)
Property income 2014/15	4,154

Answer bank

Task 5.5

Sinead's property income for 2014/15 is:

£ 4,600

	£
Property one: rent (9/12 × £8,000)	6,000
Property two: rent (4 × £450)	1,800
Less expenses on property one	(1,200)
expenses on property two	(2,000)
Property income 2014/15	4,600

Task 5.6

Suzy's property income for 2014/15 is:

£ 1,750

	£
Property income (12 × £500)	6,000
Less expenses on property	(3,700)
	2,300
Property income (12 × £500)	6,000
Less rent a room relief	(4,250)
Property income 2014/15	1,750

Suzy will elect for rent a room relief as this gives a lower assessable amount.

Task 5.7

	✓
Setting the loss of £(5,000) against her employment income in 2014/15	
Carrying forward the loss of £(5,000) against property income in 2015/16	
Setting the loss of £(5,000) first against the profit of £3,000 in 2014/15 and then carrying forward the balance of £(2,000) against property income in 2015/16	✓
Setting the loss of £(5,000) first against the profit of £3,000 in 2014/15 and then setting the balance of £(2,000) against employment income in 2014/15	

Answer bank

Task 5.8

A property can qualify as qualifying holiday accommodation if it is:

Available for letting to the public as holiday accommodation for at least 210 days in the tax year and actually let for at least 105 days during the same tax year and not normally occupied for periods of 'longer term occupation' (more than 31 consecutive days to the same person) for more than 155 days in a tax year.

Task 5.9

	✓
True	
False	✓

Losses on qualifying holiday accommodation cannot be set against other income, or property income that doesn't qualify as holiday accommodation. Losses from qualifying holiday accommodation can only be set against income from the same holiday letting business.

Task 5.10

	✓
True	
False	✓

To be qualifying holiday accommodation, the property must be situated in the EEA (which includes the UK).

Answer bank

Task 5.11

Olivia's property income loss for 2014/15 is:

£ (420)

	£
Property income (52 × £40)	2,080
Less expenses on property	(2,500)
Property income loss	(420)

Olivia will elect to set aside rent a room relief in order to give herself a property loss. Otherwise as her gross rental income does not exceed £4,250, rent a room relief would apply automatically and the income and expenses would be ignored for tax purposes.

Task 5.12

	✓
The income qualifies as earnings for pension purposes	
The wear and tear allowance applies	✓
Capital allowances are available on furniture	

The wear and tear allowance is not available in relation to furnished holiday property. Landlords of qualifying holiday accommodation use capital allowances on furniture instead.

Answer bank

Task 5.13

The property income taxable on Len for 2014/15 assuming that he uses the rent-a-room scheme is:

£90	
£430	✓
£4,316	
£4,680	

	£
Income from letting (£90 × 52)	4,680
Less rent a room relief	(4,250)
Taxable property income	430

Task 5.14

Qualifying holiday accommodation

For a property to be qualifying holiday accommodation, the property must, broadly, be:

(a) Furnished accommodation
(b) Situated in the European Economic Area
(c) Let on commercial basis with a view to realisation of profit
(d) Available for commercial letting to the public for not less than 210 days in a tax year
(e) Actually let for 105 days within the 210 day period
(f) Not more than 155 days of the tax year must fall during periods of longer term occupation. Longer term occupation is described as a continuous period of more than 31 days during which the accommodation is in the same occupation.

The income tax advantages are:

(a) The income qualifies as earnings for pension purposes.
(b) Capital allowances are available on furniture. The wear and tear allowance does not apply.

Task 5.15

Page 1
Your name   Pierce Jones
Box 1   1

Page 2
Box 20   6000.00 (£500 x 12)
Box 24   650.00 (£400 + £250)
Box 26   3200.00
Box 29   1200.00
Box 38   950.00
Box 40   950.00

Answer bank

Answer bank

Payment of tax and tax administration

Task 6.1

By which date should an individual normally submit his 2014/15 self assessment tax return if it is to be filed online?

	✓
31 January 2016	✓
5 April 2016	
31 October 2015	
31 December 2015	

Task 6.2

How will Gordon settle his income tax payable for 2014/15?

	✓
The full amount of £17,000 will be paid on 31 January 2016	
Payments on account of £7,250 will be made on 31 January and 31 July 2015, with nothing due on 31 January 2016	
Payments on account of £8,500 will be made on 31 January and 31 July 2015 with nothing due on 31 January 2016	
Payments on account of £7,250 will be made on 31 January and 31 July 2015, with the balance of £2,500 being paid on 31 January 2016	✓

Task 6.3

What is the latest date until which Pat must retain records of his income?

All records until 31 January 2017	
Property income until 31 January 2017, dividend income until 31 January 2021	
Property income until 31 January 2021, dividend income until 31 January 2017	
All records until 31 January 2021	✓

Task 6.4

The minimum penalty as a percentage of Potential Lost Revenue for a deliberate but not concealed error on a tax return, for which is there is an unprompted disclosure is:

0%	
20%	✓
30%	
35%	

Task 6.5

The maximum penalty per tax year for failing to keep records is:

£ 3,000

Task 6.6

Dear John

Income tax return

I am writing to let you know that I will need the following information and documents in order to complete your income tax return for the year to 5 April 2015:

(1) **Forms P60 and P11D**

   Both of these forms should have been supplied to you by your employer. Form P60 will give me details of your salary and tax deducted from it. Form P11D will give me the details I need regarding your company car and private medical insurance.

(2) **Bank and Building Society Certificates of annual interest earned**

   These will provide the details I need regarding your taxable interest and the tax deducted from it.

(3) **Annual pension statement**

   This will give me the details I need of your pension payments and of any tax withheld at source from the payments.

(4) **Receipted subscription notice**

   This will show me details of the subscription you have paid.

I do not need any details of either your mortgage payments or of the interest arising on your NISA account. This is because there is no tax relief for mortgage payments, and the interest arising on your NISA account is tax-free.

(a) Your completed tax return must be submitted to HMRC by 31 January 2016 providing you submit it online. If you want to file a paper return, you would need to submit it by 31 October 2015.

(b) Any outstanding tax is due for payment on 31 January 2016.

(c) A fixed penalty of £100 applies if your tax return is not submitted online by 31 January 2016. In addition, if the return is more than three months late, then a potential daily penalty of £10 per day may be imposed from then on and this can apply for up to 90 days. There is a further penalty of 5% of tax due if the return is more than six months late (minimum of £300). Another further penalty is charged if the return is more than 12 months late. This is 5% of tax due (minimum £300) unless the withholding of information is deliberate and concealed or deliberate but not concealed when it rises to 100% or 70% respectively.

   Interest is charged on a daily basis in respect of any tax paid late. There is a penalty of 5% of tax due 30 days after the due date. A further 5% penalty is charged where the tax is still unpaid at six and twelve months after the due date. This gives a maximum penalty of 15% of the unpaid tax.

(d) Finally, in response to the final point in your letter, a husband and wife are taxed independently, so there will be no need for us to consider your wife's income when completing your tax return.

Yours sincerely

Peter Jones

Answer bank

Task 6.7

From:	AATStudent@boxmail.net
To:	Dicer@hotnet.net
Sent:	1 December 2015
Subject:	Information

First, as I have submitted the tax return, we need to notify HM Revenue & Customs as soon as possible that there are omissions. However, there should be no penalties, as there should be no additional tax due. I will explain why this is the case.

On the tax return, we need to declare your gross income, which will include all sources of income, even those from which tax has already been deducted. The total tax liability is then calculated, and the tax you have already paid is deducted.

In your case, as you are not a higher or additional rate taxpayer, there will be no additional tax to pay.

For the building society interest, we need to gross it up by the 20% tax already deducted, and declare £190 (being £152 x 100/80). The income tax due on this will have been deducted by the building society before paying you the interest, and so there is no further tax to pay.

The interest from the NISA is exempt from tax, so there is no need to declare that income.

The Gift Aid donation that you paid to the National Trust would get additional tax relief if you paid tax at the higher or additional rate, but as you do not, there will be no effect.

I will inform HMRC as soon as possible on your behalf, but there should be no penalties to pay.

Task 6.8

From:	AATStudent@boxmail.net
To:	clarissa@hotnet.net
Sent:	17 September 2015
Subject:	Worried

The maximum penalty for a careless (rather than a deliberate) error is 30% of the potential lost revenue (ie tax lost). The potential lost revenue here is £420 × 20% = £84 so the maximum penalty is £25.20.

However, this may be reduced to 0% if you disclose the error to HMRC when you have no reason to believe HMRC has discovered, or is about to discover, the error. You should therefore make disclosure to HMRC as soon as possible.

Interest is payable on the £84 tax due. This will be charged from 31 January 2015 to the day before it is paid so again you should make sure that you pay it as soon as possible.

Task 6.9

The usual rules are that half of the tax liability for any year is paid by 31 January in that tax year and the other half is paid by 31 July following the tax year.

This is based on an estimate, using the preceding tax year's tax payable figure and the payments are called payments on account. A balancing payment is made on 31 January following the tax year, if required, or a repayment made by HMRC if the tax payable is less than the total of the payments on account.

Since 2014/15 was the first tax year in which you had property income, there were no payments on account and you just pay the whole liability by 31 January 2016.

However for 2015/16 you are required to make payments on account. This is based on the tax payable for 2014/15 which is why the payment required on 31 January 2016 for 2015/16 is half of £5,000, that is £2,500.

If you overpay for 2015/16, you will receive a refund from HMRC.

You can claim to reduce these payments on account as you think that your property income will not be as high as it was last year. You need to estimate what your property income will be for 2015/16, the tax that will be payable on it and then apply to reduce the payments on account to half of this amount.

But you do need to be careful because if you make an incorrect claim to reduce these payments on account, then HMRC will charge you interest on the difference between what should have been paid and what was actually paid and may also charge you a penalty if the claim was made negligently.

Answer bank

Chargeable gains

Task 7.1

For the gain on the disposal of a capital asset to be a chargeable gain there must be a chargeable

| disposal |

of a chargeable

| asset |

by a chargeable

| person |

Task 7.2

Item	Chargeable asset	Exempt asset
Car		✓
A plot of land	✓	
Jewellery	✓	
Premium bonds		✓
Government stock ('gilts')		✓

Task 7.3

	✓
The gift of an asset	
The sale of part of an asset	
The transfer of an asset on death	✓
The sale of the whole of an asset	

Answer bank

Task 7.4

	✓
£34,000	✓
£39,000	
£45,000	
£50,000	

	£
Proceeds of sale	90,000
Less cost	(40,000)
Less enhancement expenditure	(5,000)
Chargeable gain	45,000
Less annual exempt amount	(11,000)
Taxable gain	34,000

Task 7.5

(1) Lenny's capital gains tax liability for 2014/15 is:

£ 1,523

	£
Chargeable gains	20,000
Less allowable losses	(3,560)
Net chargeable gains	16,440
Less annual exempt amount	(11,000)
Taxable gains	5,440
CGT: £5,440 × 28%	1,523

(2) Lenny's capital gains tax liability is payable by:

31/01/2016

Task 7.6

Larry's capital gains tax liability for 2014/15 is:

£ 2,064

	£
Chargeable gains	25,000
Less allowable losses	(5,200)
Net chargeable gains	19,800
Less annual exempt amount	(11,000)
Taxable gains	8,800

CGT payable

£4,000 × 18%	720
£4,800 × 28%	1,344
	2,064

Task 7.7

Laura's capital gains tax liability for 2014/15 is:

£ 2,454

	£
Chargeable gains (£5,000 + £17,500)	22,500
Less allowable losses	(2,000)
Net chargeable gains	20,500
Less annual exempt amount	(11,000)
Taxable gains	9,500

CGT payable

	£
£2,065 (W) @ 18%	372
£7,435 @ 28%	2,082
	2,454

(W) Unused basic rate band is £31,865 − £29,800 = £2,065

Answer bank

Task 7.8

Lisa's capital gains tax liability for 2014/15 is:

| £ | 3,884 |

	£
Chargeable gains	27,000
Less annual exempt amount	(11,000)
Taxable gains	16,000
CGT	
£5,965 (W) @ 18%	1,074
£10,035 @ 28%	2,810
	3,884

(W) Unused basic rate band is £31,865 – £25,900 = £5,965

Task 7.9

(1) The cost of the land sold is:

| £ | 120,000 |

$$\frac{240,000}{240,000 + 60,000} \times £150,000$$

(2) The chargeable gain on sale is:

| £ | 117,000 |

	£
Disposal proceeds	240,000
Less disposal costs	(3,000)
Net proceeds	237,000
Less cost	(120,000)
Chargeable gain	117,000

124

Answer bank

Task 7.10

The full amount will be paid on 31 January 2016	✓
The full amount will be paid on 31 January 2015	
Payments on account will be made on 31 January and 31 July 2015, with the balance being paid on 31 January 2016	
Payments on account will be made on 31 January and 31 July 2014, with the balance being paid on 31 January 2015	

Task 7.11

The losses to carry forward to 2015/16 are:

£ 4,800

	£
Gains	18,200
Losses	(7,000)
	11,200
Losses b/f £(11,200 – 11,000)	(200)
	11,000
Less annual exempt amount	(11,000)
Taxable gains	NIL

Losses c/f £(5,000 – 200) = £4,800

Task 7.12

Mike's chargeable gain on sale is:

£ 7,000

	£
Proceeds of sale	16,000
Less allowable cost (value at death)	(9,000)
Chargeable gain	7,000

Answer bank

Task 7.13

Luke's chargeable gain on sale is:

£ | 17,000

	£
Proceeds of sale	25,000
Less disposal costs	(2,500)
Net proceeds of sale	22,500
Less allowable cost	
25,000/(25,000 + 50,000) × £16,500	(5,500)
Chargeable gain	17,000

Task 7.14

	✓
True	✓
False	

If an individual has allowable losses brought forward, these are only used to bring gains down to the annual exempt amount.

Answer bank

Task 7.15

The maximum allowable loss carried forward to 2015/16 will be:

£ 11,600

Tax year	2012/13	2013/14	2014/15
	£	£	£
Gains	2,000	4,000	13,400
Losses	(14,000)	(2,000)	(2,000)
Net gain/(loss)	(12,000)	2,000	11,400
Less loss b/f	(0)	0	(400)
Less annual exempt amount	0	(2,000)	(11,000)
Chargeable gain	0	0	0
Loss c/f	(12,000)	(12,000)	(11,600)

The use of the loss brought forward in 2014/15 is restricted to leave chargeable gains equal to the annual exempt amount.

Task 7.16

	✓
Mike	
Susan	
Simon	
Sarah	✓

Mary is married to Mike. Mike has a sister, Susan who is married to Simon. Susan and Simon have a daughter called Sarah. Sarah is not a connected person in relation to Mary.

Answer bank

Task 7.17

The loss of £(3,000) can be set against the gain of £5,000.

True	
False	✓

The loss of £(3,000) can only be set against gains on disposals made to the son (ie the same connected person) in the same tax year or future tax years.

Task 7.18

Her chargeable gain on sale is:

£ | 833

	£
Gross proceeds	6,500
Less costs of sale	(130)
Net proceeds	6,370
Less cost	(1,500)
Chargeable gain	4,870
Gain cannot exceed 5/3 × £(6,500 – 6,000)	833

Task 7.19

Jolyon's allowable loss is:

£ | 1,125

	£
Deemed proceeds	6,000
Less costs of sale	(125)
Net proceeds	5,875
Less cost	(7,000)
Allowable loss	(1,125)

Answer bank

Task 7.20

Rowenna has a chargeable gain on sale of £1,500.

True	
False	✓

Both the proceeds and the cost are less than £6,000 so the gain is exempt.

Task 7.21

Her chargeable gain on sale is:

£1,200	
£2,000	
£2,500	✓
£3,700	

	£
Gross proceeds	7,500
Less costs of sale	(300)
Net procceds	7,200
Less cost	(3,500)
Chargeable gain	£3,700
Gain cannot exceed 5/3 × £(7,500 – 6,000)	£2,500

Task 7.22

Mark's allowable loss is:

£	(3,500)

	£
Deemed proceeds	6,000
Less costs of sale	(500)
Net proceeds	5,500
Less cost	(9,000)
Allowable loss	(3,500)

Answer bank

Task 7.23

Box 1	Isabel Redding
Box 3	19100.00
Box 6	2500.00
Box 7	1750.00
Box 18	1
Box 19	7000.00
Box 20	9500.00
Box 21	0
Box 24	1
Box 25	5000.00
Box 26	2800.00
Box 27	2200.00
Box 30	1
Box 31	30000.00
Box 32	13100.00
Box 33	16900.00

Share disposals

Task 8.1

His net chargeable gain on sale is:

£ | 9,800

Mr Stevens will match his disposal of 5,000 shares on 10 August 2014 to acquisitions as follows:

1. 1,000 shares bought on 16 August 2014 (next 30 days, FIFO basis)
2. 4,000 shares from the share pool (which only consists of the 6,000 shares bought in July 2013)

Disposal of 1,000 shares bought on 16 August 2014

	£
Proceeds of sale £20,000 × 1,000/5,000	4,000
Less cost	(4,200)
Allowable loss	(200)

Disposal of 4,000 shares bought from the share pool (= July 2013 acquisition)

	£
Proceeds of sale £20,000 × 4,000/5,000	16,000
Less cost £9,000 × 4,000/6,000	(6,000)
Chargeable gain	10,000

Net chargeable gain = £10,000 – 200   9,800

Answer bank

Task 8.2

	✓
Against 10,000 of the shares purchased on 10 May 2007	
Against 5,000 of the shares purchased on 24 January 2015 and then against 5,000 of the shares purchased on 10 May 2007	
Against 10,000 of the total shareholding of 20,000 shares	
Against the 8,000 shares purchased on 24 January 2015 and then against 2,000 of the shares purchased on 10 May 2007	✓

Task 8.3

Share pool

	No. of shares	Cost £
10 February 2000	12,000	18,000
20 September 2007 Bonus 1:4 (1/4 × 12,000 = 3,000 shares)	3,000	0
	15,000	18,000
15 March 2015 Disposal (£18,000 × 2,000/15,000 = £2,400)	(2,000)	(2,400)
	13,000	15,600

Gain on sale

	£
Proceeds	8,000
Less cost	(2,400)
Gain	5,600

Task 8.4

Mark will match his disposal of 10,000 shares on 4 November 2014 as follows:

1. 2,000 shares bought on 10 November 2014
2. 8,000 shares from share pool

Disposal of 2,000 shares bought on 10 November 2014	£
Proceeds $\frac{2,000}{10,000} \times £60,000$	12,000
Less cost	(11,500)
Chargeable gain	500

Disposal of 8,000 shares from share pool	
Proceeds $\frac{8,000}{10,000} \times £60,000$	48,000
Less cost (W)	(12,200)
Chargeable gain	35,800

Total chargeable gain (£500 + £35,800)	36,300

Share pool working	No. of shares	Cost
		£
9 December 2000	12,000	4,400
12 October 2004 Rights 1:3 @ £5	4,000	20,000
(1/3 × 12,000 = 4,000 shares × £5 = £20,000)		
	16,000	24,400
4 November 2014 Disposal	(8,000)	(12,200)
(£24,400 × 8,000/16,000 = £12,200)		
	8,000	12,200

Answer bank

Principal private residence

Task 9.1

	✓
16.5/25	✓
8.5/25	
15.5/25	
11.5/25	

	Chargeable	Exempt
Actual occupation		8
Employment abroad (actual occupation before and after period of absence) – any period		5
Actual occupation		2
Absence (not followed by period of actual occupation)	8.5	
Last 18 months of ownership		1.5
Totals	8.5	16.5

Task 9.2

	£
Proceeds	180,000
Less cost	(50,000)
Gain before PPR exemption	130,000
Less PPR exemption (£130,000 × 10/18)	(72,222)
Chargeable gain	57,778

Answer bank

Working

	Exempt years	Chargeable years
1.8.96 – 31.7.99 (actual occupation)	3	
1.8.99 – 31.7.03 (up to 4 years due to place of work – not employed abroad)	4	
1.8.03 – 31.7.04 (up to 3 years any reason)	1	
1.8.04 – 31.1.05 (actual occupation)	½	
1.2.05 – 31.1.13 (not followed by actual occupation)		8
1.2.13 – 31.7.14 (last 1½ years)	1½	
Totals	10	8

AAT AQ2013
SAMPLE ASSESSMENT
PERSONAL TAX

Time allowed: 2 hours

Personal Tax AAT (AQ2013) sample assessment

Taxation tables for personal tax – 2014/15

Pop-up 1

Tax rates and bands

	%	£
Basic rate	20	first 31,865
Higher rate	40	to 150,000
Additional rate	45	over 150,000

Savings income is taxed at 10%, 20%, 40% and 45%.

(10% applies to a maximum of £2,880 of savings income only where non-savings income is below this limit)

Dividends are taxed at 10%, 32.5% and 37.5%.

Personal allowances

	£
Personal allowance for individuals born after 5 April 1948	10,000
Age allowance for individuals born between 6 April 1938 and 5 April 1948	10,500
Age allowance for individuals born before 6 April 1938	10,660
Income limit for age allowance	27,000

Taxation Data 2

Pop-up 2

Car benefit percentage

Emission rating for petrol engines	%
0g/km	0
1 g/km to 75g/km	5
76g/km to 94g/km	11
95g/km or more	12 + 1% for every extra 5g/km above 95g/km

Diesel engines – additional 3%

The figure for fuel is £21,700

Authorised mileage rates

First 10,000 miles	45p
Over 10,000 miles	25p

Van scale charge

	£
Charge	3,090
Private fuel provided	581

HMRC official rate 3.25%

Capital gains tax

Annual exempt amount (annual exemption)	£11,000
Tax rate	18%
Higher rate	28%

Task 1 (9 marks)

George had the use of two company cars during 2014/15. The company paid for all the running costs of the cars, including all fuel.

Details of the cars are as follows:

	Periods of use	List price £	Cost £	CO₂ emission	Type of engine
Nissan	4 months of the tax year	18,500	17,800	149g/km	Petrol
Volvo	8 months of the tax year	22,800	20,300	177g/km	Diesel

Complete the following table to show George's taxable benefit in kind for the cars for 2014/15. Show monetary answers in whole pounds.

Car		%	£
Nissan	Scale charge percentage		
	Taxable benefit on provision of the car		
	Taxable benefit on provision of fuel		
Volvo	Scale charge percentage		
	Taxable benefit on provision of the car		
	Taxable benefit on provision of fuel		
Total taxable benefit			

AAT AQ2013 sample assessment: questions

Task 2 (10 marks)

(a) Indicate whether each of the following will or will not result in an assessable benefit in kind for the employee by dragging the correct item into the answer column of the table.

The following are provided by the employer to the employee	Answer
Free parking spaces outside the place of work.	
Provision of a £11,000 interest free loan.	
Contribution of £150 per year towards employee's household costs as the employee works from home one day per week.	
Free meals provided to all directors and senior managers.	

Drag items

| Will be treated as an assessable benefit |

| Will NOT be treated as an assessable benefit |

Roweena received the following benefits during 2014/15:

1. She was provided with the use of a house that was bought by her employer in March 2006 for £214,000. The house was extended and improved in October 2010 at a cost of £18,500. In June 2014, the house was further extended at a cost of £5,400. The house has an annual value of £4,700.

2. The furniture for the house was provided by her employer at a cost of £22,000.

3. On 1 November 2012, Roweena had been given a £15,000 loan on which she paid her employer 1% interest. On 1 July 2014, Roweena repaid £3,000 of the loan, but she had made no other repayments. No elections have been made in respect of the loan.

(b) Complete the sentences below using this information.

The cost of accommodation that will be used in the benefit in kind computation will be:

£ ☐

The taxable benefit in kind arising from the accommodation will be:

£ ☐

The taxable benefit in kind arising from the provision of the furniture will be:

£ ☐

The taxable benefit in kind arising from the loan will be:

£ ☐

Task 3 (10 marks)

Barrie has a furnished house which he lets for £515 per calendar month.

His expenditure for the year was as follows:

Cost of redecoration	£1,000
Annual insurance premium from 1 January 2014	£1,800
Annual insurance premium from 1 January 2015	£2,200
Water rates	£600
Council tax	£2,150

(a) Calculate the profit or loss made on the property by inputting the correct figures in the boxes. Do not use brackets or minus signs and if you feel any items are not allowable please insert a zero '0'.

	£
Property income	
Property expenses:	
Redecoration	
Insurance	
Water rates	
Council tax	
Wear and tear	
PROFIT	

Charlene's only income is derived from the letting of property. She has profits and losses for the last few years as shown in the table below.

(b) Show how the loss made in 2013/14 would be relieved by selecting the appropriate figure from each of the drop-down lists. If you consider there to be no loss relieved in that year select the zero figure from the drop-down list.

	2012/13 £	2013/14 £	2014/15 £
Property income/(loss)	8,700	(2,200)	1,300
Loss relieved	☐	—	☐

Drop-down list:

0
(1,300)
(2,200)
(8,700)

Task 4 (6 marks)

Angela receives interest from a (new) ISA, interest from a Building Society account and dividends from shares. Her other income, net of personal allowances, totalled £29,795 for 2014/15. She has no other sources of income.

Calculate the tax deducted at source and any additional tax payable for each type of income shown in the table below. If your answer is zero, please input a '0'. Your answer should be in pounds and pence.

Income	Income received £	Tax deducted at source £	Additional tax payable £
Interest from NISA	412		
Interest from Building Society	856		
Dividends	1,314		

Task 5 (12 marks)

Kayla, who was born in September 1967, provides you with the following information that relates to her income for 2014/15:

1) Her annual salary from 1 January 2014 was £105,800. On 1 January 2015 she received a 2% pay rise.

2) She has the use of a company car, on which the benefit in kind has been computed at £3,350. The company pays for all running costs, including the fuel and this benefit in kind has been computed at £4,190.

3) She paid an annual subscription to her professional body costing £290.

4) Kayla is in the company pension scheme. She pays 6% of her salary into this scheme, and her employer pays 8% of her salary.

5) During 2014/15, Kayla received £1,080 in interest from a building society account and £380 in interest from a (new) ISA.

AAT AQ2013 sample assessment: questions

Complete the following table showing the figure that may be included in Kayla's taxable income for 2014/15. You should use whole pounds only. If your answer is zero, please input a '0'. Do not use brackets or minus signs.

	£
Salary	
Employee's pension contribution	
Employer's pension contribution	
Benefit in kind for cars	
Benefit in kind for fuel	
Professional subscription	
Interest from Building Society	
Interest from NISA	
Personal allowance	
Taxable Income	

Task 6 (10 marks)

Yubin, who is 36, has the following income for 2014/15:

	£
Total employment income	40,300
Interest received from Building Societies	1,480
Dividends received	774

(a) Calculate his total income tax liability for 2014/15, entering your answer and workings into the blank table below. You have been given more space than you will need.

Yubin is considering contributing into a private pension scheme, paying 5% of his employment income each year. However, he does not understand the taxation implications of doing this.

(b) Explain to Yubin how he will get tax relief on such contributions, and tax implications if he had paid into this scheme during 2014/15.

AAT AQ2013 sample assessment: questions

Task 7 (10 marks)

Today is 14 April 2015.

A new client has written to you explaining his situation. He has been self-employed for many years, but the last tax return he filed with HMRC was for the tax year 2012/13, which he filed on 1 October 2014. He has not filed any further returns.

He is now very worried about penalties that he may be charged.

In the box below, respond to the client's query by explaining what penalties he may incur due to the late filing of his tax returns.

Task 8 (7 marks)

Jermaine rented out two properties during 2014/15. The summary information from these properties is:

Property	Rental Income £	Repairs £	Council Tax
P – unfurnished	8,900	2,600	1,910
R – furnished	10,700	1,200	2,370

Where possible, Jermaine claims the wear and tear allowance.

Jermaine pays 8% of rents received in management fees. He had property losses of £4,300 from 2013/14.

Complete the relevant parts of the following tax return by inputting information into the boxes provided.

Property income

Do not include furnished holiday lettings, Real Estate Investment Trust or Property Authorised Investment Funds dividends/distributions here.

20 Total rents and other income from property
£ _____ . 0 0

21 Tax taken off any income in box 20
£ _____ . 0 0

22 Premiums for the grant of a lease – from box E on the Working Sheet – *read the notes*
£ _____ . 0 0

23 Reverse premiums and inducements
£ _____ . 0 0

Property expenses

24 Rent, rates, insurance, ground rents etc.
£ _____ . 0 0

25 Property repairs, maintenance and renewals
£ _____ . 0 0

26 Loan interest and other financial costs
£ _____ . 0 0

27 Legal, management and other professional fees
£ _____ . 0 0

28 Costs of services provided, including wages
£ _____ . 0 0

29 Other allowable property expenses
£ _____ . 0 0

Calculating your taxable profit or loss

30 Private use adjustment – *read the notes*
£ _____ . 0 0

31 Balancing charges – *read the notes*
£ _____ . 0 0

32 Annual Investment Allowance
£ _____ . 0 0

33 Business Premises Renovation Allowance (Assisted Areas only) – *read the notes*
£ _____ . 0 0

34 All other capital allowances
£ _____ . 0 0

35 Landlord's Energy Saving Allowance
£ _____ . 0 0

36 10% wear and tear allowance – *for furnished residential accommodation only*
£ _____ . 0 0

37 Rent a Room exempt amount
£ _____ . 0 0

38 Adjusted profit for the year – from box O on the Working Sheet – *read the notes*
£ _____ . 0 0

39 Loss brought forward used against this year's profits
£ _____ . 0 0

40 Taxable profit for the year (box 38 minus box 39)
£ _____ . 0 0

41 Adjusted loss for the year – from box O on the Working Sheet – *read the notes*
£ _____ . 0 0

42 Loss set off against 2014-15 total income – *this will be unusual – read the notes*
£ _____ . 0 0

43 Loss to carry forward to following year, including unused losses brought forward
£ _____ . 0 0

Task 9 (12 marks)

(a) Show whether the following statements are true or false.

	True	False
The destruction of a capital asset through fire would not be treated as a chargeable disposal for capital gains tax.	☐	☐
Disposals on the death of a taxpayer would be treated as exempt disposals for capital gains tax.	☐	☐
The sale of a racehorse would be treated as an exempt asset for the purposes of capital gains tax.	☐	☐
Wasting chattels are tangible movable items with an estimated life of fifty years or less.	☐	☐

Joyce bought an asset in April 2003 for £105,000, selling it in November 2014 for £148,600. Joyce paid auctioneer's commission of 7.5% when she bought the asset and auctioneer's fees of 10% on the sale value of the asset.

(b) Select the gain arising from the disposal of this asset from the list below.

£43,600 ☐

£35,725 ☐

£28,740 ☐

£20,865 ☐

Jules bought 75 acres of land in July 2005 for £112,500. In February 2015, she sold 20 acres for £85,200 when the remaining 35 acres were valued at £70,350.

(c) Complete the following table for the disposal of this land.

	Workings	£
Proceeds		☐
Cost	☐ / (☐ + ☐) × ☐	☐
Gain		☐

Task 10 (8 marks)

Jason bought 1,950 shares in Landle Ltd in May 2002 for £46,800. In September 2004, there was a 1 for 10 bonus issue. In February 2006, he sold 700 shares for £19,600. On 12 November 2014, he sold 800 shares for £25,600. On 19 November 2014, he bought 400 shares for £12,000.

Clearly showing the balance of shares and their value to carry forward, calculate the gain made on the sale of the shares in 2014/15. All workings must be shown in your calculations.

Task 11 (6 marks)

Alex bought a house on 1 March 2002 for £178,000 and sold the property on 31 October 2014 for £312,000.

During the period of ownership the following occurred:

Period	
01.03.02-31.12.04	Alex lived in the property
01.01.05-31.06.06	Alex moved in with his sick brother
01.07.06-30.06.08	Alex lived in the property
01.07.08-31.12.11	Alex worked abroad
01.01.12-31.10.14	Alex lived in the property until he sold it

(a) Input the correct answers in the boxes provided to complete the sentences. Where applicable round your answer to the nearest whole number.

The total period of ownership of the house is ☐ months.

The period of Alex's actual and deemed residence is ☐ months.

The chargeable gain on the sale of the house is £ ☐.

The capital gains for three taxpayers for 2014/15 are shown in the table below, together with their capital losses brought forward from 2013/14. The gains are before deduction of the annual exempt amount.

(b) Tick to show how much of each of the losses brought forward will be relieved in 2014/15.

	Gain 2014/15	Loss 2013/14	Relieve all loss	Relieve some loss	Relieve no loss
Huw	£43,800	£35,900	☐	☐	☐
Jason	£15,800	£3,900	☐	☐	☐
Matt	£9,900	£4,400	☐	☐	☐

AAT AQ2013
SAMPLE ASSESSMENT
PERSONAL TAX

ANSWERS

AAT AQ2013 sample assessment: answers

Personal Tax AAT (AQ2013) sample assessment

Task 1 (9 marks)

Complete the following table to show George's taxable benefit in kind for the cars for 2014/15. Show your answer in pounds only.

Car		%	£
Nissan	Scale charge percentage	22	
	Taxable benefit on provision of the car		1,357
	Taxable benefit on provision of fuel		1,591
Volvo	Scale charge percentage	31	
	Taxable benefit on provision of the car		4,712
	Taxable benefit on provision of fuel		4,485
Total taxable benefit			12,145

Nissan

The CO_2 emissions of the car are 145g/km (rounded down to the nearest five below).

Amount over baseline figure 145 – 95 = 50g/km

Divide 50 by 5 = 10

The taxable percentage is 12% + 10% = 22%

Car benefit = £18,500 (list price) × 22% × 4/12

Fuel benefit = £21,700 × 22% × 4/12

Volvo

Scale charge percentage = 175g/km (rounded down) – 95 = 80g/km /5 = 16% + 12% + 3%

Car benefit = £22,800 (list price) × 31% × 8/12

Fuel benefit = £21,700 × 31% × 8/12

AAT AQ2013 sample assessment: answers

Task 2 (10 marks)

(a) Indicate whether each of the following will or will not result in an assessable benefit in kind for the employee by dragging the correct item into the answer column of the table.

The following are provided by the employer to the employee	Answer	Options
Free parking spaces outside the place of work.	Will NOT be treated as an assessable benefit in kind	Will be treated as an assessable benefit in kind
Provision of a £11,000 interest free loan.	Will be treated as an assessable benefit in kind	Will NOT be treated as an assessable benefit in kind
Contribution of £150 per year towards employee's household costs as the employee works from home one day per week.	Will NOT be treated as an assessable benefit in kind	
Free meals provided to all directors and senior managers.	Will be treated as an assessable benefit in kind	

(b) **Complete the sentences below using this information.**

The cost of accommodation that will be used in the benefit in kind computation will be £ 232,500

(cost plus improvements to beginning of current tax year)

The taxable benefit in kind arising from the accommodation will be £ 9,818

(£4,700 + (£232,500 – £75,000) × 3.25%))

The taxable benefit in kind arising from the provision of the furniture will be £ 4,400

(£22,000 × 20%)

The taxable benefit in kind arising from the loan will be £ 304

(£15,000 + £12,000)/2 = £13,500 × 2.25% (3.25 – 1)

Tutorial note

The strict method produces a benefit in kind of

(£15,000 × 2.25% × 3/12) + (£12,000 × 2.25% × 9/12) = £287

154

Task 3 (10 marks)

(a) Calculate the profit or loss made on the property by inputting the correct figures in the boxes. Do not use brackets or minus signs and if you feel any items are not allowable please insert a zero '0'.

	£
Property income (£515 × 12)	6,180
Property expenses:	
Redecoration	1,000
Insurance (£1,800 × 9/12) + (£2,200 × 3/12)	1,900
Water rates	600
Council tax	2,150
Wear and tear (£6,180 – £600 – £2,150) × 10%	343
PROFIT	187

Charlene's only income is derived from the letting of property. She has profits and losses for the last few years as shown in the table below.

(b) Show how the loss made in 2013/14 would be relieved by selecting the appropriate figure from each of the drop-down lists. If you consider there to be no loss relieved in that year select the zero figure from the drop-down list.

	2012/13 £	2013/14 £	2014/15 £
Property income/(loss)	8,700	(2,200)	1,300
Loss relieved	0	–	(1,300)

Task 4 (6 marks)

Angela receives interest from an ISA, interest from a Building Society account and dividends from shares. Her other income, net of personal allowances, totalled £29,795 for 2014/15. She has no other sources of income.

Calculate the tax deducted at source and any additional tax payable for each type of income shown in the table below. If your answer is zero, please input a '0'. Your answer should be in pounds and pence.

Income	Income received £	Tax deducted at source £	Additional tax payable £
Interest from NISA	412	0	0 (Exempt income)
Interest from Building Society	856	214 (£856 × 20/80)	0 (Gross income of £1,070 fall in basic rate band)
Dividends	1,314	146 (£1,314 × 10/90)	103.50 (Gross income = £1,460. £1,000 falls in basic rate band and £460 taxed at 22.5% (32.5 – 10))

Task 5 (12 marks)

Complete the following table showing the figure that may be included in Kayla's taxable income for 2014/15. You should use whole pounds only. If your answer is zero, please input a '0'. Do not use brackets or minus signs.

	£
Salary (£105,800 × 9/12) + (£105,800 × 102% × 3/12)	106,329
Employee's pension contribution (6% × £106,329)	6,380
Employers pension contribution	0
Benefit in kind for cars	3,350
Benefit in kind for fuel	4,190
Professional subscription	290
Interest from Building Society (£1,080 × 100/80)	1,350
Interest from NISA	0
Total income	108,549
Personal allowance £(10,000 – 4,274 (108,549 – 100,000)/2))	5,726
Taxable income	102,823

Task 6 (10 marks)

Yubin, who is 36, has the following income for 2014/15:

	£
Total employment income	40,300
Interest received from Building Societies	1,480
Dividends received	774

(a) Calculate his total income tax liability for 2014/15, entering your answer and workings into the blank table below. You have been given more space than you will need.

	Workings	£
Employment income		40,300
Building society interest	£1,480 × 100/80	1,850
Dividends	£774 × 100/90	860
		43,010
Personal allowance		10,000
		33,010
£30,300 × 20%	£(40,300 – 10,000)	6,060
£1,565 × 20%	£(31,865 – 30,300)	313
£285 × 40%	£(1,850 – 1,565)	114
£860 × 32.5%		280
Total		6,767

Yubin is considering contributing into a private pension scheme, paying 5% of his employment income each year. However, he does not understand the taxation implications of doing this.

(b) Explain to Yubin how he will get tax relief on such contributions, and tax implications if he had paid into this scheme during 2014/15.

If Yubin contributes 5% of his employment income into a personal pension scheme, this will total £2,015. This amount will be grossed up for the basic rate, giving a total of £2,519. This amount is then used to extend the basic rate of income tax, so that he would not pay the higher rate until his taxable income was £34,384 (31,865 + 2,519). This would therefore mean that all his income for 2014/15 would be taxable at the basic rate.

AAT AQ2013 sample assessment: answers

Task 7 (10 marks)

Today is 14th April 2015.

A new client has written to you explaining his situation. He has been self-employed for many years, but the last tax return he filed with HMRC was for the tax year 2012/13, which he filed on 1 October 2014. He has not filed any further returns.

He is now very worried about penalties that he may be charged.

In the box below you need to respond to the client's query by explaining what penalties he may incur due to late filing of his tax returns.

> The 2012/13 tax return should have been filed by 31 January 2014. The client filed it 8 months late and so he will incur a penalty. This penalty may consist of: an immediate £100 fine; a daily penalty of £10 per day to a maximum of £900; penalty of £300 or 5% of the tax liability for the year.
>
> The 2013/14 tax return was also due to be filed by 31 January 2015, so by 14th April, this is 2½ months late. An immediate fine of £100 will be due, but provided he files it before 30th April 2015, he should avoid further penalties.

Task 8 (7 marks)

Box 20: 19,600

Box 24: 4,280

Box 25: 3,800

Box 27: 1,568 (19,600 × 8%)

Box 36: 833 (10,700 – 2370 × 10%)

Box 38: 9,119

Box 39: 4,300

Box 40: 4,819

AAT AQ2013 sample assessment: answers

Task 9 (12 marks)

(a) Show whether the following statements are true or false.

	True	False
The destruction of a capital asset through fire would not be treated as a chargeable disposal for capital gains tax.		✓
Disposals on the death of a taxpayer would be treated as exempt disposals for capital gains tax.	✓	
The sale of a racehorse would be treated as an exempt asset for the purposes of capital gains tax.	✓	
Wasting chattels are tangible movable items with an estimated life of fifty years or less.	✓	

Joyce bought an asset in April 2003 for £105,000, selling it in November 2014 for £148,600. Joyce paid auctioneers commission of 7.5% when she bought the asset and auctioneer's fees of 10% on the sale value of the asset.

(b) Select the gain arising from the disposal of this asset from the list below.

£43,600 ☐

£35,725 ☐

£28,740 ☐

£20,865 ✓

Proceeds	£148,600 – £14,860 =	£133,740
Less cost	£105,000 + £7,875 =	(£112,875)
Gain		£20,865

Jules bought 75 acres of land in July 2005 for £112,500. In February 2015, she sold 40 acres for £85,200 when the remaining 35 acres were valued at £70,350.

(c) Complete the following table for the disposal of this land.

	Workings £	£
Proceeds		85,200
Cost	$\dfrac{85,200}{85,200 + 70,350} \times 112,500$	61,620
Gain		23,580

Note: Under the costs workings on the second line, the answer 85,200 + 70,360 may also be written in as 70,350 + 85,200

AAT AQ2013 sample assessment: answers

Task 10 (8 marks)

Kyn bought 1,950 shares in Landle Ltd in May 2002 for £46,800. In September 2004, there was a 1 for 10 bonus issue. In February 2006, he sold 700 shares for £19,600. On 12 November 2014, he sold 800 shares for £25,600. On 19 November 2014, he bought 400 shares for £12,000.

Clearly showing the balance of shares and their value to carry forward, calculate the gain made on the sale of the shares in 2014/15. All workings must be shown in your calculations.

	Event	Shares	£
May 2002	Purchase	1,950	46,800
September 2004	Bonus issue	195	
		2,145	
February 2006	Disposal	(700)	(15,273)
		1,445	31,527
November 2014	Disposal	(400)	(8,727)
		1,045	22,800
		Next 30 days (400)	Share pool (400)
Proceeds		12,800	12,800
Cost		12,000	8,727
		800	4,073
Total gain	£800 + £4,073		4,873

Task 11 (6 marks)

Alex bought a house on 1 March 2002 for £178,000 and sold the property on 31 October 2014 for £312,000.
During the period of ownership the following occurred:

Period	
01.03.02-31.12.04	Alex lived in the property
01.01.05-31.06.06	Alex moved in with his sick brother
01.07.06-30.06.08	Alex lived in the property
01.07.08-31.12.11	Alex worked abroad
01.01.12-31.10.14	Alex lived in the property until he sold it

(a) Input the correct answers in the boxes provided to complete the sentences. Where applicable round your answer to the nearest whole number.

The total period of ownership of the house is [152] months.

The period of Alex's actual and deemed residence [152] months.

The chargeable gain on the sale of the house is £ [0].

The capital gains for three taxpayers for 2014/15 are shown in the table below, together with their capital losses brought forward from 2013/14. The gains are before deduction of the annual exempt amount.

(b) Tick to show how much of each of the losses brought forward will be relieved in 2014/15.

Taxpayer	Gain 2014/15	Loss 2013/14	Relieve all loss	Relieve some loss	Relieve no loss
Danny	£43,800	£35,900	☐	✓	☐
Daniel	£15,800	£3,900	✓	☐	☐
Danielle	£9,900	£4,400	☐	☐	✓

BPP PRACTICE ASSESSMENT 1
PERSONAL TAX

Time allowed: 2 hours

Personal Tax BPP practice assessment 1

Taxation tables for personal tax – 2014/15

Note that 'TAXATION DATA 1' and 'TAXATION DATA 2' shown below will be available as pop-up windows throughout your live assessment.

TAXATION DATA 1
Pop-up 1
Tax rates and bands

	%	£
Basic rate	20	first 31,865
Higher rate	40	to 150,000
Additional rate	45	over 150,000

Savings income is taxed at 10%, 20%, 40% and 45%
(10% applies to a maximum of £2,880 of savings income only where non-savings income is below this limit.)

Dividends are taxed at 10%, 32.5% and 37.5%.

Personal allowances

	£
Personal allowance for individuals born after 5 April 1948	10,000
Age allowance for individuals born between 6 April 1938 and 5 April 1948	10,500
Age allowance for individuals born before 6 April 1938	10,660
Income limit for age allowance	27,000

TAXATION DATA 2
Pop-up 2

Car benefit percentage

Emission rating for petrol engines	%
0g/km	0
1g/km to 75g/km	5
76g/km to 94g/km	11
95g/km or more	12% + 1% for every extra 5g/km above 95g/km

Diesel engines – additional 3%

The figure for fuel is £21,700

Authorised mileage rates

First 10,000 miles	45p
Over 10,000 miles	25p

Van scale charge

	£
Charge	3,090
Private fuel provided	581

HMRC official rate   3.25%

Capital gains tax

Annual exempt amount	£11,000
Tax rate	18%
Higher rate	28%

Task 1

Shane is provided with a company car for business and private use throughout 2014/15. The car had a list price of £16,700 when bought new in December 2012, although the company paid £15,000 for the car after a dealer discount. It has a petrol engine, with CO_2 emissions of 154g/km. The company pays for all running costs, including all fuel. Shane does not make any contribution for his private use of the car.

(1) The cost of the car in the taxable benefit computation is:

£ ☐

(2) The percentage used in the taxable benefit computation is:

☐ %

(3) The taxable benefit in respect of the provision of fuel for private use is:

£ ☐

Task 2

(a) Josie is a basic rate taxpayer and receives the following benefits as the result of her employment.

In each case enter the taxable benefit arising in 2014/15. If the benefit is exempt, enter 0.

(1) A mobile telephone for private and business use throughout the year. The purchase of the phone and the calls from it cost her employer a total of £350 for 2014/15.

£ ☐

(2) Childcare vouchers of £100 per week for 48 weeks during 2014/15.

£ ☐

(3) Leisure club membership for Josie costing £5,000 using a corporate discount scheme. If a member of the public had taken this membership it would have cost £6,500.

£ ☐

(4) Use of a house near her work that enables her to start work at 7.00am every morning. The house has an annual value of £5,900 and cost her employer £227,000 4 years ago.

£ ☐

BPP practice assessment 1: questions

(b) For each of the following benefits, tick whether they would be wholly or partly taxable or wholly exempt if received in 2014/15:

Item	Wholly or partly taxable	Wholly exempt
Interest on loan of £8,000 (only loan provided)	☐	☐
Additional costs of home working of £5 per week (no evidence presented to employer)	☐	☐
Use of pool car	☐	☐
One staff party costing £120 per head	☐	☐

Task 3

(a) Emily lets a furnished house for £150 a week. During 2014/15 the flat was let for 40 weeks. It was unoccupied for the remaining 12 weeks of the year.

During 2014/15, Emily spent £190 on advertising for tenants, £460 on water rates, £800 on redecoration, £690 on electricity and £368 on cleaning. Emily also installed a new central heating system at a cost of £1,200. She claims the wear and tear allowance where possible.

Calculate the property income taxable on Emily for 2014/15 using the proforma layout provided. Fill in all the unshaded boxes. If any item is not an allowable expense, enter 0. Both brackets and minus signs can be used to show negative numbers.

Rent	
Expenses:	
Advertising	
Water rates	
Redecoration	
Electricity	
Cleaning	
Central heating system	
Wear and tear	
Property income	

(b) Oliver and George jointly own a house, which is their main residence. They let out one of the rooms to Julie.

What is the maximum exempt amount to which Oliver and George are each entitled under rent a room relief?

	✓
£2,000	
£2,125	
£4,000	
£4,250	

Task 4

During 2014/15, Eva received the following income.

In each case, show the amount of income that she should enter on her tax return. If the income is exempt, enter 0.

(1) Employment income £20,000, tax deducted £2,700.

£ ☐

(2) NS&I investment account interest £40.

£ ☐

(3) Interest on NISA account £90.

£ ☐

(4) Dividends received £1,152.

£ ☐

Task 5

Denise works for Jules Ltd. She provides you with the following information:

(1) Annual salary £104,000 received on 25th day of each month

(2) Employer's contribution of 5% of salary on 31 December 2014 to company's occupational pension scheme. Denise contributes 4% of her salary into this scheme.

(3) Bonus of £1,000 received 30 April 2014 based on company's accounting profit for the year ended 31 December 2013

(4) Bonus of £1,200 received 30 April 2015 based on company's accounting profit for the year ended 31 December 2014

(5) She has use of a company car for which the benefit in kind has been computed as £3,000. Denise pays for all the private petrol that she uses in this car.

(6) During 2014/15 Denise received £120 of bank interest and £50 of dividends from a new ISA.

Complete the following table showing the figures that should be included in Denise's taxable income for 2014/15. You should use whole pounds only. If your answer is zero, please input a '0'. Do not use brackets or minus signs.

	£
Salary	
Employer's pension contribution	
Employee's pension contribution	
Bonus received 30 April 2014	
Bonus received 30 April 2015	
Benefit in kind for car	
Interest from bank	
Dividends from NISA	
Total income	
Personal allowance	
Taxable income	

Task 6

(a) Elaine was born in 1968. During 2014/15 she earned £115,000 of employment income and received bank interest of £20,000 and dividends of £18,000.

Calculate her total income tax liability to the nearest pound for 2014/15, entering your answer and workings in the blank table given below. You have been given more space than you will need.

(b) Elaine is considering making a Gift Aid donation of £500 each year to a charity. However she does not understand the tax implications of doing this.

Explain to Elaine how she will get tax relief on such donations, and the tax implications if she had made a £500 Gift Aid donation during 2014/15.

Task 7

Today's date is 15 January 2016.

Margaret filed her 2013/14 tax return online on 25 November 2015.

The assessment for 2013/14 showed a tax liability of £800, which has not yet been paid.

Discuss the penalties and interest that may be applied by HMRC on Margaret for both the late filing of the tax return and the late payment of tax. Explain how any outstanding tax for 2014/15 may be collected by HMRC, based on the information given above.

Task 8

Sarah Cartney owns a bungalow that she rents out for £500 per calendar month, payable on the first day of each month. The property is let unfurnished. She pays an agency 10% of the gross rent to run the letting for her. She paid £1,250 in water rates during 2014/15. Sarah made an allowable loss of £860 on this rental in 2013/14.

Using this information complete the property income page.

Property income

Do not include furnished holiday lettings, Real Estate Investment Trust or Property Authorised Investment Funds dividends/distributions here.

20 Total rents and other income from property

21 Tax taken off any income in box 20

22 Premiums for the grant of a lease – form box E on the Working Sheet – *read the notes*

23 Reverse premiums and inducements

Property expenses

24 Rent, rates, insurance, ground rents etc.

25 Property repairs, maintenance and renewals

26 Loan interest and other financial costs

27 Legal, management and other professional fees

28 Costs of services provided, including wages

29 Other allowable property expenses

Calculating your taxable profit or loss

30 **Private use adjustments** – *read the notes*

31 Balancing charges – *read the notes*

32 Annual Investment Allowance

33 Business Premises Renovation Allowance (Assisted Areas only) – *read the notes*

34 All other capital allowances

35 Landlord's Energy Saving Allowance

36 10% wear and tear allowance – *for furnished residential accommodation only*

37 Rent a Room exempt amount

38 Adjusted profit for the year – from box O on the Working Sheet – *read the notes*

39 Loss brought forward used against this year's profits

40 Taxable profit for the year (box 38 minus box 39)

41 Adjusted loss for the year – from box O on the Working Sheet – *read the notes*

42 Loss set off against 2014-15 total income – *this will be unusual – read the notes*

43 Loss to carry forward to following year, including unused losses brought forward

Task 9

(a) For each of the following assets, tick whether they are chargeable or exempt assets for capital gains tax:

Asset	Chargeable	Exempt
Car used solely for business purposes	☐	☐
Holiday cottage	☐	☐
Vintage car worth £40,000	☐	☐
Shares held in a new individual savings account	☐	☐

(b) Rodney purchased an antique chair for £1,450. On 10 October 2014 he sold the chair at auction for £6,300 (which was net of the auctioneer's 10% commission).

The chargeable gain on sale is:

£ ☐

(c) Andrew bought six acres of land for £405,000. He sold two acres of the land at auction for £360,000. His disposal costs were £6,000. The market value of the four remaining acres at the date of sale was £540,000.

(1) **The cost of the land sold is:**

£ ☐

(2) **The chargeable gain on sale is:**

£ ☐

Task 10

In August 2009 Wayne acquired 4,000 shares in Main plc at a cost of £10,000. In September 2011, there was a one for one bonus issue when the shares were worth £8 each. Wayne sold 3,000 shares in July 2012 for £15,000, and purchased 3,000 back again October 2012 for 12,000.

Wayne sold half of his shareholding in June 2014 for £21,000.

Clearly showing the balance of shares and their value to carry forward, calculate the gain made on the sale of the shares in 2014/15. All workings must be shown in your calculations.

Task 11

(a) **For each of the following statements, tick if they are True or False.**

Any CGT annual exempt amount that is unused in one tax year can be carried forward to be used in the following tax year only.

True ☐

False ☐

Capital losses in a tax year must be offset against capital gains in that year, even if it means losing all, or some of the annual exempt amount.

True ☐

False ☐

(b) Charlotte bought a house on 1 February 2002 for £95,000 and sold it for £263,000 on 1 October 2014. During the period of ownership the following occurred:

01.02.02 to 31.10.04	Charlotte lived in the property
01.11.04 to 31.03.13	Charlotte worked elsewhere in the UK
01.04.13 to 31.09.14	Charlotte lived in the property until she sold it

Input the correct answers in the boxes provided to complete the sentences. Where applicable round your answer to the nearest whole number.

The total period of ownership of the property is ☐ months.

The period of Charlotte's actual and deemed residence is ☐ months.

The chargeable gain on the sale of the house is ☐.

(c) Ella purchased an antique clock for £12,000. She sold it on 1 September 2014 for £62,000. Ella has no other chargeable assets. Her taxable income for 2014/15 was £29,465.

Ella's CGT payable for 2014/15 is:

£ ☐

This is payable by (xx/xx/xxxx):

☐

BPP PRACTICE ASSESSMENT 1
PERSONAL TAX

ANSWERS

BPP practice assessment 1: answers

Personal Tax BPP practice assessment 1

Task 1

(1) The cost of the car in the taxable benefit computation is:

£ 16,700

(2) The percentage used in the taxable benefit computation is:

23 %

(150 – 95)/5 = 11% + 12% = 23%

(3) The taxable benefit in respect of the provision of fuel for private use is:

£ 4,991

£21,700 × 23%

Task 2

(a)

(1) Mobile telephone

£ 0

(2) Childcare vouchers

£ 2,160

£(100 – 55) × 48

(3) Leisure club membership (cost to employer)

£ 5,000

(4) Home (£5,900 + ((£227,000 – 75,000) × 3.25%))

£ 10,840

(b)

Item	Wholly or partly taxable	Wholly exempt
Interest on loan of £8,000 (only loan provided)		✓ (£10,000 or less)
Additional costs of home working of £5 per week (no evidence presented to employer)	✓ (evidence needed if more than £4 per week)	
Use of pool car		✓
One staff party costing £120 per head		✓ (up to £150)

Task 3

(a)

	£
Rent accrued £150 × 40	6,000
Expenses:	
Advertising	(190)
Water rates	(460)
Redecoration	(800)
Electricity	(690)
Cleaning	(368)
Central heating system (capital)	(0)
Wear and tear £(6,000 − 460) × 10%	(554)
Property income	2,938

(b)

	✓
£2,000	
£2,125	✓
£4,000	
£4,250	

The rent a room limit of £4,250 is halved if any other person also receives income from renting accommodation in the property.

Task 4

(1) Employment income £20,000, tax deducted £2,700.

| £ | 20,000 |

(2) NS&I investment account interest £40 (received gross).

| £ | 40 |

(3) Interest on NISA account £90.

| £ | 0 |

Exempt

(4) Dividends received £1,152.

| £ | 1,280 |

£1,152 × 100/90

Task 5

	£
Salary	104,000
Employer's pension contribution (exempt)	0
Employee's pension contribution (£104,000 × 4%)	4,160
Bonus received 30 April 2014	1,000
Bonus received 30 April 2015	0
Benefit in kind for car	3,000
Interest from bank (£120 × 100/80)	150
Dividends from NISA (exempt)	0
Total income	103,990
Personal allowance £(10,000 – 1,995 (103,990 – 100,000)/2)	8,005
Taxable income	95,985

Task 6

(a)

	Non-savings £	Interest £	Dividends £
Employment Income	115,000		
Bank interest (£20,000 × 100/80)		25,000	
Dividends (£18,000 × 100/90)			20,000
Net income	115,000	25,000	20,000
Personal allowance (net income > £120,000)	(nil)		
Taxable income	115,000	25,000	20,000

£31,865 × 20%	6,373
£83,135 (£115,000 – £31,865) × 40%	33,254
£25,000 × 40%	10,000
£10,000 × 32.5%	3,250
£10,000 × 37.5%	3,750
Income tax liability	56,627

(b)

If you make a Gift Aid donation of £500 each year to charity this amount will be grossed up at the basic rate of tax, giving a gross amount of £625.

This gross figure of £625 will be used to extend the upper limit of the basic rate band to give an upper limit of £32,490 (£31,865 + £625).

This would mean that an extra £625 of your employment income would be taxed at the basic rate of tax of 20% instead of at the higher rate of tax of 40%.

Task 7

Late return

Firstly, the return should have been filed by 31 January 2015. Margaret would receive an immediate fine of £100 for missing this date. As the return is more than three months late, HMRC may then charge a penalty of £10 per day (up to a maximum of 90 days) while the return is outstanding. As the return is also more than six months late, another penalty may arise which is the greater of £300 or 5% of the tax liability for the year.

Late payment

The £800 should have been paid by 31 January 2015. Interest would be incurred from the due date of payment to the actual date of payment. A penalty will also be imposed, being 10% of the tax outstanding as it is more than six months late.

2014/15

For 2014/15, as the income tax payable for 2013/14 is less than £1,000, payments on account will not be required. Instead, the tax for 2014/15 will all be due on 31 January 2016.

Task 8

Box 20 (£500 × 12)	6000.00
Box 24	1250.00
Box 27 (£6,000 × 10%)	600.00
Box 38	4150.00
Box 39	860.00
Box 40	3290.00

Task 9

(a)

Asset	Chargeable	Exempt
Car used solely for business purposes		✓
Holiday cottage	✓	
Vintage car worth £40,000		✓
Shares held in a new individual savings account		✓

(b)

The chargeable gain on sale is:

£ 1,667

	£
Disposal proceeds £6,300 × 100/90	7,000
Less disposal costs £7,000 × 10%	(700)
Net proceeds	6,300
Less cost	(1,450)
Gain	4,850
Cannot exceed 5/3 × £(7,000 – 6,000)	1,667

(c)

(1) The cost of the land sold is:

£ 162,000

$$\frac{360,000}{360,000 + 540,000} \times £405,000$$

(2) The chargeable gain on sale is:

£ 192,000

	£
Disposal proceeds	360,000
Less disposal costs	(6,000)
Net proceeds	354,000
Less cost	(162,000)
Chargeable gain	192,000

Task 10

	£
Proceeds of sale	21,000
Less cost	(9,125)
Gain	11,875

	No. of shares	Cost £
August 2009 Acquisition	4,000	10,000
September 2011 Bonus 1 for 1	4,000	nil
	8,000	10,000
July 2012 Disposal (3,000/8,000 × £10,000)	(3,000)	(3,750)
	5,000	6,250
October 2012 Acquisition	3,000	12,000
	8,000	18,250
June 2014 Disposal (4,000/8,000 × £18,250)	(4,000)	(9,125)
c/f	4,000	9,125

Task 11

(a)

True ☐
False ☑

Any unused annual exempt amount is lost.

True ☑
False ☐

Only capital losses brought forward can be restricted to ensure the annual exempt amount isn't lost.

(b)

The total period of ownership of the property is | 152 | months.

The period of Charlotte's actual and deemed residence is | 135 | months.

01.02.02 – 31.10.04	33 months actual occupation
01.11.04 – 31.03.13	48 months – deemed occupation – working elsewhere in UK – preceded and followed by actual occupation
	36 months – deemed occupation – any reason – preceded and followed by actual occupation
	18 months non-occupation
01.04.13 – 31.09.14	18 months – actual occupation (last 18 months always deemed occupation anyway)

The chargeable gain on the sale of the house is | £18,789 |.

	£
Disposal proceeds	263,000
Less cost	(95,000)
	168,000
PPR £168,000 × 135/152	(149,211)
Chargeable gain	18,789

(c)

Ella's CGT payable for 2014/15 is:

£ 10,680

This is payable by:

31/01/2016

	£
Disposal proceeds	62,000
Less cost	(12,000)
Gain	50,000
Less annual exempt amount	(11,000)
Taxable gain	39,000
CGT	
On £2,400 @ 18% (unused basic rate band £31,865 – £29,465)	432
On £36,600 @ 28%	10,248
	10,680

BPP practice assessment 1: answers

BPP PRACTICE ASSESSMENT 2
PERSONAL TAX

Time allowed: 2 hours

BPP practice assessment 2: questions

Personal Tax BPP practice assessment 2

TAXATION DATA

Taxation tables for personal tax – 2014/15

Note that 'TAXATION DATA 1' and 'TAXATION DATA 2' shown below will be available as pop-up windows throughout your live assessment.

TAXATION DATA 1
Pop-up 1

Tax rates and bands

	%	£
Basic rate	20	first 31,865
Higher rate	40	to 150,000
Additional rate	45	over 150,000

Savings income is taxed at 10%, 20%, 40% and 45%
(10% applies to a maximum of £2,880 of savings income only where non-savings income is below this limit.)

Dividends are taxed at 10%, 32.5% and 37.5%.

Personal allowances

	£
Personal allowance for individuals born after 5 April 1948	10,000
Age allowance for individuals born between 6 April 1938 and 5 April 1948	10,500
Age allowance for individuals born before 6 April 1938	10,660
Income limit for age allowance	27,000

TAXATION DATA 2
Pop-up 2

Car benefit percentage

Emission rating for petrol engines	%
0g/km	0
1g/km to 75g/km	5
76g/km to 94g/km	11
95g/km or more	12% + 1% for every extra 5g/km above 95g/km

Diesel engines – additional 3%

The figure for fuel is £21,700

Authorised mileage rates

First 10,000 miles	45p
Over 10,000 miles	25p

Van scale charge

	£
Charge	3,090
Private fuel provided	581

HMRC official rate   3.25%

Capital gains tax

Annual exempt amount	£11,000
Tax rate	18%
Higher rate	28%

BPP practice assessment 2: questions

Task 1

Steel Ltd provides Susan with two company cars during 2014/15 for private and business use. The first car cost £13,800 when new, has CO_2 emissions of 130g/km and has a diesel engine. The second car has a list price of £12,000, has CO_2 emissions of 90g/km and has a petrol engine. Susan used the first car for the first 7 months of 2014/15, and the second car for the remaining 5 months. Steel Ltd pays for all the running costs which amount to £950 for the first car and £735 for the second car. Steel also paid for private fuel for the second car, however Susan had to contribute £20 per month towards this.

(1) The scale charge percentage for the first car is:

[ ] %

(2) The taxable benefit for the first car is:

£ [ ]

(3) The scale charge percentage for the second car is:

[ ] %

(4) The taxable benefit for the second car is:

£ [ ]

(5) The fuel benefit for the second car is:

£ [ ]

Task 2

(a) Which ONE of the following is not a wholly exempt employment benefit?

	✓
Long service award of £900 to employee with 30 years of service	
Workplace parking	
Workplace childcare facilities	
Moving expenses of £10,000	

(b) For each of the following benefits provided to Emily by her employer Bloom Ltd, calculate the amount of the taxable benefit for 2014/15. If a benefit is exempt, enter 0.

(1) Bloom Ltd gave Emily a loan on 1 August 2014 of £6,000 to pay for home improvements. Emily pays the company 1.25% interest on the loan, but has not repaid any of the loan itself.

BPP practice assessment 2: questions

The taxable benefit for 2014/15 is:

£ [ ]

(2) On 1 May 2014 Bloom Ltd provided her with a mobile telephone costing £150 for private and business use.

The taxable benefit for 2014/15 is:

£ [ ]

(c)

Bella's employer provided her with a house on 1 April 2014, when it was valued at £125,000. The employer had bought the house for £80,000 on 1 April 2005. The annual value of the house is £1,500. Bella pays £75 a month to the employer for the use of the house. She is also provided with new furniture valued at £15,000 on 1 April 2014.

(1) **The basic accommodation benefit for 2014/15 is:**

£ [ ]

(2) **The cost of providing the accommodation for calculating the additional benefit is:**

£ [ ]

(3) **The additional accommodation benefit for 2014/15 is:**

£ [ ]

(4) **The benefit for provision of furniture for 2014/15 is:**

£ [ ]

Task 3

(a)

Demi bought two properties on 1 July 2014.

Property 1 was let unfurnished from 1 September 2014 at an annual rent of £12,000 payable monthly in arrears. The rent due on 31 March 2015 was not received until 14 April 2015.

The following were expenses paid by Demi on the property:

		£
1 July 2014	Insurance for the year ended 30 June 2015	700
8 Sept 2014	Accountancy fees	100
25 January 2015	Re-painting the exterior of the property	400

Property 2 was let furnished from 1 August 2014 at an annual rent of £9,000 payable annually in advance.

The following were expenses paid by Demi on the property:

		£
1 July 2014	Insurance for the year ended 30 June 2015	800
31 March 2015	Redecoration	900

Using the proforma layout provided, calculate Demi's property income for the tax year 2014/15 by filling in the unshaded boxes. Add zeros if necessary. Both brackets and minus signs can be used to show negative numbers.

	Property 1	Property 2
	£	£
Rental income		
Property 1		
Property 2		
Less expenses		
Insurance		
Accountancy		
Repainting		
Redecoration		
Wear and tear allowance		
Net income		
Rental income		

(b)

Which ONE of the following is not a condition for a property to be qualifying holiday accommodation?

	✓
The property is furnished	
The property must be actually let for at least 105 days during the same tax year	
The property must be available for letting to the public as holiday accommodation for at least 210 days in the tax year	
The property must be situated in the UK	

Task 4

Sarah receives a dividend of £7,200 on 10 December 2014.

(1) **The gross amount of the dividend is:**

£ ☐

(2) **The tax credit attaching to the dividend is:**

£ ☐

(3) **Sarah will receive a repayment if the tax credit exceeds her income tax liability**

True ☐

False ☐

Paul receives interest of £5,000 from a NISA and £3,500 from building society interest during 2014/15.

(4) **His gross amount of savings income for 2014/15 is:**

£ ☐

(5) **The tax deducted at source is:**

£ ☐

(6) **Paul will receive a repayment of the tax deducted at source if it exceeds his income tax liability**

True ☐

False ☐

Task 5

(a)

Gavin is employed by XYZ plc. For each of the following payments, state the amount of employment income taxable in 2014/15. If an amount is not taxable in 2014/15 enter 0.

(1) Annual salary received in monthly payments on the last working day of each month. Until the end of December 2014, his annual salary was £36,000. He had a 2% annual pay increase with effect from 1 January 2015.

The salary to be included in employment income for 2014/15 is:

£ ☐

(2) Bonus of £2,000 received 31 March 2015 based on company's accounting profit for the year ended 31 December 2014.

The bonus to be included in employment income for 2014/15 is:

£ ☐

(3) Commission of £500 received 30 April 2015 on sales made in the month of March 2015.

The commission to be included in employment income for 2014/15 is:

£ ☐

(4) Employer's contribution of £5,000 on 10 March 2015 towards Gavin's occupational pension scheme.

The benefit to be included in employment income for 2014/15 is:

£ ☐

(b)

Your client Jackie, who was born in March 1969, received the following income in 2014/15:

	£
Trading income	20,000
Property income	5,000
Building society interest	116
Interest from NS&I investment account	180
Interest from a NISA	204
Dividends	189

(1) **Jackie's total non-savings income for 2014/15 is:**

£ ☐

(2) **Jackie's total savings income for 2014/15 is:**

£ ▢

(3) **Jackie's total dividend income for 2014/15 is:**

£ ▢

Task 6

(a)

Donald has the following amounts of taxable income for 2014/15:

Non-savings income £152,395 (PAYE deducted £52,000)
Savings income £145 (Tax deducted at source £29)
Dividend income £210 (Tax credit £21)

Donald's tax liability on each source of income for 2014/15 is as follows:

(1) **Non-savings income:**

£ ▢

(2) **Savings income:**

£ ▢

(3) **Dividend income:**

£ ▢

(4) **Donald's tax payable for 2014/15 is:**

£ ▢

(b)

You have received the following email from Serena Miles:

From:	SMiles@webmail.net
To:	AATStudent@boxmail.net
Sent:	30 November 2015
Subject:	Pensions

I currently don't have a pension and I am worried about this. I have two options. My employer, ABC plc, has said that I can join their occupational pension scheme. This would involve me paying 5% of my basic salary, and they would pay another 7%. However, I don't know how long I am going to continue to work for them.

Alternatively, I am thinking of taking out a private pension, possibly paying about 6% of my earnings into it.

However, I have no idea about the tax implications of these schemes. Would I get tax relief, and if so, how?

I hope you can help.

Serena

WITHOUT discussing the merits of each scheme, advise Serena on the tax implications of an occupational pension scheme and a private pension scheme.

From:	AATStudent@boxmail.net
To:	SMiles@webmail.net
Sent:	1 December 2015
Subject:	Pensions

Task 7

Julie has income tax payable for 2014/15 of £4,215. She was not required to make any payments on account.

(1) **The date by which the tax payable should be paid is:** (insert date as xx/xx/xxxx)

[   ]

(2) **Each payment on account for 2015/16 is:**

£ [   ] . [   ]

(3) **The dates by which the payments on account for 2015/16 should be paid are:** (insert dates as xx/xx/xxxx)

[   ]

and

[   ]

(4) Julie is a higher rate taxpayer. She has omitted to include £1,500 of building society income (gross) in her return for 2014/15.

Assuming that the error is a deliberate error without concealment but Julie makes disclosure of the error without prompting, the minimum penalty for error that will be imposed is:

£ [   ]

Task 8

You act for Ricky Fernandez, who is employed by PQR plc. He has provided you with the following information about his employment in 2014/15:

	PQR plc £
Salary paid	30,000
Tax taken off	4,700
Company car benefit	4,500
Fuel benefit	2,400
Professional subscription paid by Ricky	300

Using this information complete the employment income page.

HM Revenue & Customs

Employment
Tax year 6 April 2014 to 5 April 2015

Your name

Your unique taxpayer reference (UTR)

Complete an *Employment* page for each employment or directorship

1. Pay from this employment - the total from your P45 or P60 - *before tax was taken off*
   £ . 0 0

2. UK tax taken off pay in box 1
   £ . 0 0

3. Tips and other payments not on your P60 - *read page EN 3 of the notes*
   £ . 0 0

4. PAYE tax reference of your employer (on your P45/P60)

5. Your employer's name

6. If you were a company director, put 'X' in the box

7. And, if the company was a close company, put 'X' in the box

8. If you are a part-time teacher in England or Wales and are on the Repayment of Teachers' Loans Scheme for this employment, put 'X' in the box

Benefits from your employment - use your form P11D (or equivalent information)

9. Company cars and vans - *the total 'cash equivalent' amount*
   £ . 0 0

10. Fuel for company cars and vans - *the total 'cash equivalent' amount*
    £ . 0 0

11. Private medical and dental insurance - *the total 'cash equivalent' amount*
    £ . 0 0

12. Vouchers, credit cards and excess mileage allowance
    £ . 0 0

13. Goods and other assets provided by your employer - *the total value or amount*
    £ . 0 0

14. Accommodation provided by your employer - *the total value or amount*
    £ . 0 0

15. Other benefits (including interest-free and low interest loans) - *the total 'cash equivalent' amount*
    £ . 0 0

16. Expenses payments received and balancing charges
    £ . 0 0

Employment expenses

17. Business travel and subsistence expenses
    £ . 0 0

18. Fixed deductions for expenses
    £ . 0 0

19. Professional fees and subscriptions
    £ . 0 0

20. Other expenses and capital allowances
    £ . 0 0

ⓘ **Shares schemes, employment lump sums, compensation, deductions and Seafarers' Earnings Deduction** are on the *Additional information* pages enclosed in the tax return pack

SA102 2014   Tax return: Employment: Page E 1   HMRC 12/13

Task 9

(a)

Classify whether a disposal of each of the following assets will be chargeable to or exempt from capital gains tax:

Asset	Chargeable	Exempt
Shares in XYZ plc held in a NISA	☐	☐
Ruby necklace valued at £100,000	☐	☐
Vintage Rolls Royce Car	☐	☐
Factory used in a trade	☐	☐

(b)

Trevor bought a 5 acre plot of land for £50,000. He sold 3 acres of the land at auction for £105,000 in August 2014. He had spent £2,500 installing drainage on the 3 acres which he sold. His disposal costs were £1,500. The market value of the remaining 2 acres at the date of sale was £45,000.

The gain on sale of the 3 acres is:

	✓
£66,000	
£66,750	
£71,000	
£66,152	

(c)

(1) Matt bought a picture for £7,000 and had costs of acquisition of £300. He sold it in August 2014 for £4,500 and had costs of disposal of £200.

The allowable loss on sale is: (either show the loss by using brackets or a minus sign)

£ ☐

BPP practice assessment 2: questions

(2) Keith bought a greyhound for £5,000. It won a number of races and he sold it for £7,000 in December 2014, incurring costs of disposal of £250.

The chargeable gain on sale is:

	✓
Nil	
£1,667	
£1,250	
£1,750	

Task 10

Lee had the following transactions in shares in Snowy Ltd:

Acquisitions	No of shares	Cost £
December 2005	10,000	10,800
August 2006	Bonus, 1 for 1	Nil
June 2010	10,000	8,700
December 2010	Rights Issue, 1 for 10	40p each
Disposal		Proceeds £
September 2014	15,000	18,650

Using the proforma layout provided, calculate the chargeable gain made on the disposal of the shares in Snowy Ltd, and show the balance of shares to be carried forward for future disposal. Fill in all unshaded boxes, enter 0 if appropriate. Both brackets and minus signs can be used to show negative numbers.

Gain

	£
Proceeds of sale	
Less cost	
Chargeable gain	

Share pool

	No of shares	Cost £
December 2005 Acquisition		
August 2006 Bonus issue		
June 2010 Acquisition		
December 2010 Rights issue		
September 2014 Disposal		
c/f		

Task 11

Irma had the following chargeable gains in 2014/15:

Gain on sale of shares August 2014	£9,241
Gain on sale of furniture February 2015	£4,167

She had allowable losses brought forward of £1,000.

Irma is an additional rate taxpayer.

(1) **Irma's taxable gains for 2014/15 are:**

£ ☐

(2) **Irma's CGT payable for 2014/15 is:**

£ ☐

(3) **Irma's CGT is due for payment by: (enter date as xx/xx/xxxx)**

☐

BPP PRACTICE ASSESSMENT 2
PERSONAL TAX

ANSWERS

BPP practice assessment 2: answers

Personal Tax BPP practice assessment 2

Task 1

(1) The scale charge percentage for the first car is:

| 22 | % |

130g/km − 95g/km = 35/5 = 7% + 12% + 3%

(2) The taxable benefit for the first car is:

| £ | 1,771 |

£13,800 × 22% × 7/12

(3) The scale charge percentage for the second car is:

| 11 | % |

(Between 76g/km and 94g/km)

(4) The taxable benefit for the second car is:

| £ | 550 |

£12,000 × 11% × 5/12

(5) The fuel benefit for the second car is:

| £ | 995 |

£21,700 × 11% × 5/12

Task 2

(a)

	✓
Long service award of £900 to employee with 30 years of service	
Workplace parking	
Workplace childcare facilities	
Moving expenses of £10,000	✓

Moving expenses of £10,000 are only exempt to the extent of £8,000.

The long service award is wholly exempt as it is within the limit of £50 for each year of service and the period of service is in excess of 20 years.

(b)

(1) The taxable benefit for 2014/15 is:

| £ | 80 |

£6,000 × (3.25% − 1.25%) × 8/12

(2) The taxable benefit for 2014/15 is:

| £ | 0 |

Exempt

(c)

(1) The basic accommodation benefit for 2014/15 is:

| £ | 600 |

	£
Annual value	1,500
Less payment by employee £75 × 12 =	(900)
Basic accommodation benefit	600

(2) The cost of providing the accommodation for calculating the additional benefit is:

| £ | 125,000 |

Cost of providing accommodation
Market value at provision (acquired more than 6 years before provision)

(3) The additional accommodation benefit for 2014/15 is:

| £ | 1,625 |

Excess of £125,000 over £75,000 = £50,000 × 3.25%

(4) The benefit for provision of furniture for 2014/15 is:

| £ | 3,000 |

£15,000 × 20%

Task 3

(a)

	Property 1 £	Property 2 £
Rental income		
Property 1 £12,000 × 7/12	7,000	
Property 2 £9,000 × 8/12		6,000
Less expenses		
Insurance £700 / £800 × 9/12	(525)	(600)
Accountancy	(100)	0
Repainting	(400)	0
Redecoration	0	(900)
Wear and tear allowance £6,000 × 10%	0	(600)
Net income	5,975	3,900
Rental income		9,875

(b)

	✓
The property is furnished	
The property must be actually let for at least 105 days during the same tax year	
The property must be available for letting to the public as holiday accommodation for at least 210 days in the tax year	
The property must be situated in the UK	✓

The property must be situated in the European Economic Area (which includes the UK).

Task 4

(1) The gross amount of the dividend is:

£ | 8,000

£7,200 × 100/90

(2) The tax credit attaching to the dividend is:

£ | 800

£8,000 × 10%

(3) True ☐

False ✓

The tax credit can only be used to reduce Sarah's tax liability to nil, and cannot be repaid.

(4) His gross amount of savings income for 2014/15 is:

£ | 4,375

£3,500 × 100/80 = £4,375. NISA interest is exempt income

(5) The tax deducted at source is:

£ | 875

£4,375 × 20%

(6) Paul will receive a repayment of the tax deducted at source if it exceeds his income tax liability

True ✓

False ☐

Task 5

(a)

(1)

The salary to be included in employment income for 2014/15 is:

| £ | 36,180 |

	£
Salary April to December 2014 9/12 × £36,000	27,000
Salary January to March 2015 3/12 × £(36,000 × 102%)	9,180

(2)

The bonus to be included in employment income for 2014/15 is:

| £ | 2,000 |

Bonus received 31 March 2015

(3)

The commission to be included in employment income for 2014/15 is:

| £ | 0 |

Commission received 30 April 2015 (taxable 2015/16)

(4)

The benefit to be included in employment income for 2014/15 is:

| £ | 0 |

Exempt benefit

(b)

(1) Jackie's total non-savings income for 2014/15 is:

| £ | 25,000 |

(2) Jackie's total savings income for 2014/15 is:

| £ | 325 |

(£116 × 100/80) + £180 = £325

BPP practice assessment 2: answers

(3) Jackie's total dividend income for 2014/15 is:

| £ | 210 |

£189 × 100/90

	Non-savings income £	Savings income £	Dividend income £
Trading income	20,000		
Property income	5,000		
Building society interest (£116 × 100/80)		145	
NS&I interest		180	
ISA interest		0	
Dividends (£189 × 100 / 90)			210
Total income	25,000	325	210

Task 6

(a)

(1) Non-savings income:

| £ | 54,705 |

	£
£31,865 × 20%	6,373
£118,135 × 40%	47,254
£2,395 × 45%	1,078
£152,395	54,705

(2) Savings income:

| £ | 65 |

£145 × 45%

(3) Dividend income:

| £ | 79 |

£210 × 37.5%

(4) Donald's tax payable for 2014/15 is:

| £ | 2,799 |

	£
Income tax liability £(54,705 + 65 + 79)	54,849
Less dividend tax credit	(21)
Interest: tax deducted at source	(29)
PAYE	(52,000)
Income tax payable	2,799

(b)

From:	AATStudent@boxmail.net
To:	SMiles@webmail.net
Sent:	1 December 2015
Subject:	Pensions

Occupational pension schemes operate by the employer deducting your pension contribution from your salary before the PAYE is calculated. In your case this would be 5%. This means that full tax relief is automatically obtained at source at your applicable rate of tax. The employer is responsible for paying over the pension payments to the pension provider.

The 7% that your employer pays to the pension scheme on your behalf has no tax implications for you, ie this will not be classed as a taxable benefit.

Private pension schemes work quite differently. You pay the pension provider direct, usually monthly. The amount you pay is net of basic rate tax.

So if for example, you decide you would like to put £100 a month into your pension, you only actually have to pay in £80, HM Revenue & Customs will pay the other £20. This automatically provides you with 20% tax relief.

If however, you are a higher or additional rate taxpayer, you will be entitled to further tax relief. In order to get tax relief at the higher rate of 40% or the additional rate of 45%, the basic rate band is extended by the gross pension contributions so that the 40% and 45% tax rates will apply after the pension has been adjusted for.

BPP practice assessment 2: answers

Task 7

(1) The date by which the tax payable should be paid is:

| 31/01/2016 |

(2) Each payment on account for 2015/16 is:

| £ | 2,107 | . | 50 |

£4,215 ÷ 2

(3) The dates by which the payments on account for 2015/16 should be paid are:

| 31/01/2016 |

and

| 31/07/2016 |

(4) Potential lost revenue £1,500 × 20% = £300 (20% tax already suffered at source)

Minimum penalty for deliberate, not concealed error with unprompted disclosure is:

| £ | 60 |

20% × £300

Task 8

Name	Ricky Fernandez
Box 1	30000.00
Box 2	4700.00
Box 5	PQR plc
Box 9	4500.00
Box 10	2400.00
Box 19	300.00

Task 9

(a)

Asset	Chargeable	Exempt
Shares in XYZ plc held in a NISA		✓
Ruby necklace valued at £100,000	✓	
Vintage Rolls Royce Car		✓
Factory used in a trade	✓	

(b)

	✓
£66,000	✓
£66,750	
£71,000	
£66,152	

	£
Proceeds of sale	105,000
Less costs of disposal	(1,500)
Net proceeds	103,500
Less cost	
(105,000/105,000 + 45,000) × £50,000	(35,000)
enhancement expenditure	(2,500)
Chargeable gain	66,000

(c)

(1) The allowable loss on sale is:

£	(1,500)

	£
Deemed disposal proceeds	6,000
Less costs of disposal	(200)
Net deemed disposal proceeds	5,800
Less cost £(7,000 + 300)	(7,300)
Allowable loss	(1,500)

BPP practice assessment 2: answers

(2)

	✓
Nil	✓
£1,667	
£1,250	
£1,750	

The greyhound is a wasting chattel and so is an exempt asset. Therefore there is no chargeable gain on the disposal.

Task 10

Gain

	£
Proceeds of sale	18,650
Less cost	(9,409)
Chargeable gain	9,241

Share pool

	No of shares	Cost £
December 2005 Acquisition	10,000	10,800
August 2006 Bonus 1 for 1	10,000	0
	20,000	10,800
June 2010 Acquisition	10,000	8,700
	30,000	19,500
December 2010 Rights 1 for 10 @ £0.40	3,000	1,200
	33,000	20,700
September 2014 Disposal (15,000/33,000 × £20,700)	(15,000)	(9,409)
c/f	18,000	11,291

218

Task 11

(1) Irma's taxable gains for 2014/15 are:

£ | 1,408

	£
Gain on shares	9,241
Gain on furniture	4,167
	13,408
Less loss brought forward	(1,000)
Net chargeable gains	12,408
Less annual exempt amount	(11,000)
Taxable gains	1,408

(2) Irma's CGT payable for 2014/15 is:

£ | 394

£1,408 × 28%

(3) Irma's CGT is due for payment by:

31/01/2016

BPP practice assessment 2: answers

BPP PRACTICE ASSESSMENT 3
PERSONAL TAX

Time allowed: 2 hours

Personal Tax BPP practice assessment 3

TAXATION DATA

Taxation tables for personal tax – 2014/15

Note that 'TAXATION DATA 1' and 'TAXATION DATA 2' shown below will be available as pop up windows throughout your live assessment.

TAXATION DATA 1
Pop-up 1

Tax rates and bands

	%	£
Basic rate	20	first 31,865
Higher rate	40	to 150,000
Additional rate	45	over 150,000

Savings income is taxed at 10%, 20%, 40% and 45%
(10% applies to a maximum of £2,880 of savings income only where non-savings income is below this limit.)

Dividends are taxed at 10%, 32.5% and 37.5%.

Personal allowances

	£
Personal allowance for individuals born after 5 April 1948	10,000
Age allowance for individuals born between 6 April 1938 and 5 April 1948	10,500
Age allowance for individuals born before 6 April 1938	10,660
Income limit for age allowance	27,000

TAXATION DATA 2
Pop-up 2

Car benefit percentage

Emission rating for petrol engines	%
0g/km	0
1g/km to 75g/km	5
76g/km to 94g/km	11
95g/km or more	12% + 1% for every extra 5g/km above 95g/km

Diesel engines – additional 3%

The figure for fuel is £21,700

Authorised mileage rates

First 10,000 miles	45p
Over 10,000 miles	25p

Van scale charge

	£
Charge	3,090
Private fuel provided	581

HMRC official rate 3.25%

Capital gains tax

Annual exempt amount	£11,000
Tax rate	18%
Higher rate	28%

Task 1

Khalid works for KML plc, and is provided with a company car for business and private use from 6 June 2014.

The car has a diesel engine with CO_2 emissions of 172g/km. It has a list price of £27,000, although the company actually paid £23,500 for the car. Khalid agreed to make a capital contribution of £6,000 towards the cost of the car. The company pays for all running costs, including all fuel. Khalid pays £50 a month towards the cost of private fuel – the actual cost of private fuel is about £90 a month.

(1) The cost of the car in the taxable benefit computation is:

	✓
£21,000	
£22,000	
£17,500	
£18,500	

(2) The percentage used in the taxable benefit computation is:

%

(3) The taxable benefit in respect of the provision of fuel for private use is:

£

Task 2

(a)

Lou is employed by Jane Quentin and receives the following benefits as the result of her employment.

In each case enter the taxable benefit arising. Enter 0 if the benefit is not taxable.

(1) An interest free loan of £10,500 made on 1 July 2014, no repayments made during 2014/15

£

(2) Cash voucher for £100 provided in December 2014. Jane acquired the voucher for £90

£

(3) Van for business and private use from 1 October 2014 onwards

£

(4) Fuel for van for private use from 1 January 2015 onwards

£

(b)

For each of the following benefits, tick whether they would be partly exempt or wholly exempt if received by an employee who is a basic rate taxpayer in 2014/15:

Benefit	Partly exempt	Wholly exempt
Staff party costing £125 per head	☐	☐
Childcare vouchers of £55 per week	☐	☐
Removal expenses of £10,000	☐	☐
Work related training costing £1,500	☐	☐

(c)

Madge is employed by V plc. She uses her own car for business purposes and is reimbursed 45p per mile by her employer. Madge travelled 15,000 miles on business in 2014/15.

What are the employment income consequences of the reimbursement for business mileage?

	✓
£6,750 taxable benefit	
£1,000 taxable benefit	
No taxable benefit or allowable deduction	
£1,000 allowable deduction	

Task 3

(a)

Michaela rents out a house from 1 July 2014.

She charges a rent of £600 per month payable in arrears on the last day of each month. The tenants don't pay the rent due on 31 March 2015 until 10 April 2015.

Michaela also pays an insurance premium of £400 on 6 July 2014, covering the period 6 July 2014 to 5 July 2015.

(1) **The rental income taxable for 2014/15 is:**

£ _____

(2) **The insurance premium allowable as an expense for 2014/15 is:**

£ [ ]

(b)

Wilma owns two flats that she rents out. Flat A is unfurnished. Flat B is furnished. The income and expenses for these properties are:

	Flat A £	Flat B £
Monthly income:		
Rent	500	650
Annual expenses:		
Council tax	1,000	800
Water rates	300	300
Insurance	350	250

Flat A was fully occupied during 2014/15. However, the tenants in Flat B moved out in November 2014, having paid the rent to the end of that month. Wilma was unable to re-let the flat until June 2015.

Wilma claims the wear and tear allowance as appropriate.

Wilma had a loss of £1,200 on her income from property in 2013/14.

Using the proforma layout below, calculate Wilma's property income for 2014/15. Fill in all unshaded boxes, enter 0 if appropriate. Both brackets and minus signs can be used to show negative numbers.

	Flat A £	Flat B £
Income		
Expenses:		
Council tax		
Water rates		
Insurance		
Wear and tear		
Net income from property		
Total property income		
Less loss b/f		
Taxable property income		

(c)

Olga owns two furnished cottages which she lets out as follows:

	Blue Cottage	Green Cottage
Days available for letting in 2014/15	195	255
Days actually let in 2014/15	106	100

Tick to show which of the properties could be qualifying holiday accommodation.

	✓
Blue Cottage only	
Green Cottage only	
Both Blue Cottage and Green Cottage	
Neither Blue Cottage nor Green Cottage	

Task 4

(a)

Using the proforma layout provided, show whether the following amounts of interest are received net of basic rate tax or gross by an individual taxpayer:

Loan stock from company
Building society fixed rate bond
NS&I Direct Saver account
Government loan stock ('gilts')

Received net	Received gross

(b)

Tick the relevant box to show which of the following types of income are chargeable to income tax and which are exempt from income tax:

Source of income	Chargeable	Exempt
New Individual Savings Account interest	☐	☐
NS&I Savings Certificates	☐	☐
Dividends received from a New Individual Savings Account	☐	☐
NS&I investment account interest	☐	☐

Task 5

(a)

The following amounts were received in relation to employment:

(a) Monthly salary of £1,500 paid on the last working day of each month

(b) Tips of £300 paid by customers directly to an employee

(c) Employer's contribution of 6% of salary to company's occupational pension scheme

(d) Reimbursement of business expenses of £500 – a dispensation is in force for such payments

For each item, tick either taxable or not taxable:

Item	Taxable	Not taxable
Salary	☐	☐
Tips	☐	☐
Employer's pension contribution	☐	☐
Reimbursement of business expenses	☐	☐

(b)

Eric Wright was born September 1959 and is employed as an architect. His employment income for 2014/15 was £96,870 and PAYE of £28,500 was deducted at source.

Eric has a bank account with the Halifax Bank. His account was credited with interest of £1,600 on 31 March 2015.

Eric received a dividend of £6,750 on 1 July 2014.

Eric made a Gift Aid donation of £400 to Oxfam on 1 December 2014.

Using the proforma layout provided, prepare a schedule of Eric's taxable income for 2014/15, clearly showing the distinction between non-savings, savings and dividend income. Both brackets and minus signs can be used to show negative numbers.

	Non-Savings income	Savings income	Dividend income	Total
	£	£	£	£

Task 6

(a)

Guy was born on 14 March 1978 and has the following income for 2014/15:

	£
Employment income (PAYE £250)	11,250
Interest received from building societies	37,000
Dividends received	12,500

Calculate Guy's income tax payable for 2014/15 entering your answer and workings into the blank table below. Brackets or a minus sign are both acceptable when entering negative numbers.

(b)

Guy is considering asking his employer to set up a small charitable donation of about £50 a month and deduct it out of his salary, but is unsure if he will get any tax relief for this.

Explain to Guy how he will get tax relief on such donations.

Task 7

(a) Owen is employed by X Ltd throughout 2014/15. He earns £35,000 a year. He also receives interest income from Santander Bank.

Until what date does Owen have to retain his records for tax for 2014/15?

	✓
All records until 31 January 2017	
Employment record until 31 January 2017, interest record until 31 January 2021	
Employment record until 31 January 2021, interest record until 31 January 2017	
All records until 31 January 2021	

(b)

You receive the following email from a client, who is a higher rate taxpayer.

From:	Raman99@sherbet.net
To:	AATStudent@boxmail.net
Sent:	20 June 2015
Subject:	More information

Hello, I am so sorry, I know that you have already sent in my tax form for 2014/15. Unfortunately, I have forgotten to tell you that I made payments of £3,000 into my personal pension scheme.

Will I have to a pay a penalty for filing an incorrect return? What is the effect on my tax liability for 2014/15?

I hope you can help me, as I feel rather worried.

Thanks.

Raman

Reply to Raman's email.

From:	AATStudent@boxmail.net
To:	Raman99@sherbet.net
Sent:	22 June 2015
Subject:	More information

Task 8

Your client, Kara Allen, has given you the following information about her capital gains position for 2014/15:

Asset sold	Proceeds	Cost
Listed shares in OPQ plc	£10,000	£8,000
Unlisted shares in K Ltd	£15,500	£16,000
Painting	£17,000	£4,000

She also had losses brought forward from 2013/14 of £7,700.

Using this information, complete the capital gains summary on the next page.

Capital gains summary
Tax year 6 April 2014 to 5 April 2015

HM Revenue & Customs

| 1 | Your name | 2 | Your Unique Taxpayer Reference (UTR) |

Summary of your enclosed computations

Please read the *Capital gains summary notes* before filling in this section. **You must enclose your computations, including details of each gain or loss, as well as filling in the boxes.**

To get notes and helpsheets that will help you fill in this form, go to hmrc.gov.uk/selfassessmentforms

3 Total gains *(Boxes 21 + 27 + 33 + 34)*
£ · 0 0

4 Gains qualifying for Entrepreneurs' Relief (but excluding gains deferred from before 23 June 2010) – *read the notes*
£ · 0 0

5 Gains invested under Seed Enterprise Investment Scheme and qualifying for exemption – *read the notes*
£ · 0 0

6 Total losses of the year – *enter '0' if there are none*
£ · 0 0

7 Losses brought forward and used in the year
£ · 0 0

8 Adjustment to Capital Gains Tax – *read the notes*
£ · 0 0

9 Additional liability for non-resident or dual resident trusts
£ · 0 0

10 Losses available to be carried forward to later years
£ · 0 0

11 Losses used against an earlier year's gain (special circumstances apply – *read the notes*)
£ · 0 0

12 Losses used against income – amount claimed against 2014-15 income – *read the notes*
£ · 0 0

13 Amount in box 12 relating to shares to which Enterprise Investment Scheme/Seed Enterprise Investment Scheme relief is attributable
£ · 0 0

14 Losses used against income – amount claimed against 2013-14 income – *read the notes*
£ · 0 0

15 Amount in box 14 relating to shares to which Enterprise Investment Scheme/Seed Enterprise Investment Scheme relief is attributable
£ · 0 0

16 Income losses of 2014-15 set against gains
£ · 0 0

17 Deferred gains from before 23 June 2010 qualifying for Entrepreneurs' Relief
£ · 0 0

BPP practice assessment 3: questions

Listed shares and securities

18 Number of disposals - *read the notes*

19 Disposal proceeds
£

20 Allowable costs (including purchase price)
£

21 Gains in the year, before losses
£

22 If you are making any claim or election, put 'X' in the box

23 If your computations include any estimates or valuations, put 'X' in the box

Unlisted shares and securities

24 Number of disposals - *read the notes*

25 Disposal proceeds
£

26 Allowable costs (including purchase price)
£

27 Gains in the year, before losses
£

28 If you are making any claim or election, put 'X' in the box

29 If your computations include any estimates or valuations, put 'X' in the box

Property and other assets and gains

30 Number of disposals

31 Disposal proceeds
£

32 Allowable costs (including purchase price)
£

33 Gains in the year, before losses
£

34 Attributed gains where personal losses cannot be set off
£

35 If you are making any claim or election, put 'X' in the box

36 If your computations include any estimates or valuations, put 'X' in the box

Any other information

37 Please give any other information in this space

SA108 2014   Page CG 2

Task 9

(a)

For each statement, tick the appropriate box in respect of the capital gains calculation:

Disposal	Market value used	Actual proceeds used	No gain/no loss disposal
Olivia sells shares for £5,000 to her wife Lucy when they are worth £4,000	☐	☐	☐
William sells land to his brother for £10,000 when it is worth £50,000	☐	☐	☐
Zeta gives an asset worth £4,000 to her friend Tanya	☐	☐	☐
Olwyn sells listed shares for proceeds of £12,000	☐	☐	☐

(b)

Melly bought a holiday cottage for £32,000, incurring legal costs of £600 on the purchase. She spent £6,000 on adding a conservatory to the cottage. This was destroyed during a storm in 2012 and not replaced. Melly sold the cottage in March 2015 for £45,000. She paid estate agent's fees of £900 and legal costs of £350.

The chargeable gain on sale is:

£ ☐

(c)

(1) Suki purchased a vase for £9,500. In December 2014 she sold the vase at auction for £2,500. This amount is before deducting the auctioneer's 10% commission.

The allowable loss on sale is:

	✓
£3,750	
£3,500	
£7,000	
£7,250	

(2) A chattel with a useful life of 60 years or less is a wasting chattel.

True ☐

False ☐

Task 10

Vernon sold 4,000 shares in R Ltd for £36,200 on 23 February 2015. He had acquired his holdings in R Ltd as follows:

Date	Transaction	No of shares	£
14 April 2000	Purchase	6,000	18,400
29 May 2005	Rights issue	1 for 20	£4 each
10 March 2015	Purchase	500	3,400

Using the proforma layout provided, compute the total gain on sale. Both brackets and minus signs can be used to show negative numbers.

Share pool

	No of shares	Cost £

Total gain on sale

	£

Task 11

(1)

Desmond bought a house in Glasgow on 1 April 2000. He lived in the house until 30 September 2003. He was then sent to work in Bristol by his employer, before returning to live in the house again on 1 October 2008. He lived in the house before moving out on 30 April 2009 to live with friends until the house was sold on 30 September 2014.

Using the proforma layout provided, show which periods of ownership are exempt and which are chargeable matching the correct explanation for each period.

Picklist for explanation:	Picklist for dates:
Not occupied and not followed by actual occupation	1 October 2003 to 30 September 2007
Actual occupation	1 May 2009 to 31 March 2013
Actual occupation	1 April 2000 to 30 September 2003
Last 18 months ownership	1 October 2007 to 30 September 2008
Up to three years any reason	1 April 2013 to 30 September 2014
Four years employed elsewhere in UK	1 October 2008 to 30 April 2009

Explanation	Exempt (dates)	Chargeable (dates)

(2) Desmond purchased the property for £210,000 on 1 April 2000, and received disposal proceeds of £385,000 on 30 September 2014. It is his main residence.

After applying principle private residence relief, the sale of Desmond's house will result in a chargeable gain.

True ☐

False ☐

(3)

If any capital gains tax is payable on the sale of his house, by what date must Desmond pay this? (xx/xx/xxxx)

BPP PRACTICE ASSESSMENT 3
PERSONAL TAX

ANSWERS

BPP practice assessment 3: answers

Personal Tax BPP practice assessment 3

Task 1

(1) The cost of the car in the taxable benefit computation is:

£21,000	
£22,000	✓
£17,500	
£18,500	

List price £27,000 less capital paid by employee (max) £5,000

(2) The percentage used in the taxable benefit computation is:

| 30 | % |

170 – 95 = 75

75 ÷ 5 = 15%

12% + 15% + 3% (diesel) = 30%

(3) The taxable benefit in respect of the provision of fuel for private use is:

| £ | 5,425 |

£21,700 × 30% × 10/12 (There is no reduction for part reimbursement of private fuel).

Task 2

(a)

(1)

| £ | 256 |

£10,500 × 3.25% × 9/12

(2)

| £ | 100 |

(3)

| £ | 1,545 |

£3,090 × 6/12

BPP practice assessment 3: answers

(4)

| £ | 145 |

£581 × 3/12

(b)

Benefit	Partly exempt	Wholly exempt
Staff party costing £125 per head		✓
Childcare vouchers of £55 per week		✓
Removal expenses of £10,000	✓ (up to £8,000)	
Work related training costing £1,500		✓

(c)

	✓
£6,750 taxable benefit	
£1,000 taxable benefit	✓
No taxable benefit or allowable deduction	
£1,000 allowable deduction	

	£
Amount reimbursed 15,000 × 45p	6,750
Less statutory allowance	
10,000 miles @ 45p	(4,500)
5,000 miles @ 25p	(1,250)
Taxable benefit	1,000

Task 3

(a)

(1) The rental income taxable for 2014/15 is:

| £ | 5,400 |

Rental income accrued 2014/15:

1 July 2014 to 31 March 2015 (working in whole months)

9 months @ £600 per month

The actual date of receipt of the rent due on 31 March 2015 is not relevant.

(2) The insurance premium allowable as an expense for 2014/15 is:

| £ | 300 |

£400 × 9/12

(b)

	Flat A £	Flat B £
Income: £500 × 12/ £650 × 8	6,000	5,200
Expenses:		
Council tax	(1,000)	(800)
Water rates	(300)	(300)
Insurance	(350)	(250)
Wear and tear £(5,200 – 800 – 300) = £4,100 × 10%	(0)	(410)
Net income from property	4,350	3,440
Total property income £(4,350 + 3,440)	7,790	
Less loss b/f	(1,200)	
Taxable property income	6,590	

BPP practice assessment 3: answers

(c)

	✓
Blue Cottage only	
Green Cottage only	
Both Blue Cottage and Green Cottage	
Neither Blue Cottage nor Green Cottage	✓

The accommodation must be available for letting to the public as holiday accommodation for at least 210 days in the tax year (Blue Cottage fails this test) and actually let for at least 105 days during the same tax year (Green Cottage fails this test).

Tutorial note

It is possible to aggregate the periods of actual letting to give an average period for each property in order to satisfy the 105 day test, but this is not relevant here because the aggregate period is less than 210 days. The availability for letting condition must be satisfied independently for each property.

Task 4

(a)

Received net	Received gross
Building society fixed rate bond	NS&I Direct Saver account
Loan stock from company	Government loan stock ('gilts')

(b)

Source of income	Chargeable	Exempt
New Individual Savings Account interest		✓
NS&I Savings Certificates		✓
Dividends received from a New Individual Savings Account		✓
NS&I investment account interest	✓	

Task 5

(a)

Item	Taxable	Not taxable
Salary	✓	
Tips	✓	
Employer's pension contribution		✓
Reimbursement of business expenses		✓

(b)

	Non-savings income £	Savings income £	Dividend income £	Total £
Employment income	96,870			
Bank interest £1,600 × 100/80		2,000		
Dividends £6,750 × 100/90			7,500	
Net income	96,870	2,000	7,500	106,370
Less: personal allowance	(7,065)			(7,065)
Taxable income	89,805	2,000	7,500	99,305

Workings

	£
Personal allowance	10,000
Less half excess (see below)	(2,935)
	7,065
Total net income	106,370
Adjustment for Gift Aid donation £400 × 100/80	(500)
Adjusted net income	105,870
Less income limit	(100,000)
Excess	5,870

247

Task 6

(a)

	Non savings income	Savings income	Dividend income
	£	£	£
Employment income	11,250		
Building society interest (£37,000 × 100/80)		46,250	
Dividends (£12,500 × 100/90)			13,889
Personal allowance	(10,000)		
Taxable income	1,250	46,250	13,889
Income tax			
£1,250 × 20%			250
£1,630 (£2,880 – £1,250) × 10%			163
£28,985 (£31,865 – £2,880) × 20%			5,797
£15,635 (£46,250 – £28,985 – £1,630) × 40%			6,254
£13,889 × 32.5%			4,514
Income tax liability			16,978
Less tax credit on dividend (313,889 × 10%)			(1,389)
Less tax deducted at source:			
Building society interest (£46,250 × 20%)			(9,250)
PAYE			(250)
Income tax payable			6,089

(b) Guy's employer will deduct the donation from his salary before it is taxed. If he decides to pay £50 a month, this will mean he will get tax relief during the year on £600 (£50 × 12), reducing his tax liability by £120 (£600 × 20%).

Task 7

(a)

	✓
All records until 31 January 2017	✓
Employment record until 31 January 2017, interest record until 31 January 2021	
Employment record until 31 January 2021, interest record until 31 January 2017	
All records until 31 January 2021	

(b)

From:	AATStudent@boxmail.net
To:	Raman99@sherbet.net
Sent:	22 June 2015
Subject:	More information

Although you have made an error in your tax return, there is no loss of tax to HMRC for reasons I will explain below. Therefore no penalty is chargeable. However, you will still need to inform HMRC by amending your tax return.

With regards to the £3,000 pension payment, you are entitled to further tax relief. The gross payment is £3,000 × 100/80 = £3,750 because you are treated as making the payment net of 20% tax.

As you are a higher rate taxpayer, you are entitled to additional tax relief on this amount. The basic rate band of £31,895 is extended by £3,750, so that the 40% tax rate will not start until the first £35,645 has been taxed at the basic rates. This will therefore reduce the amount of tax you need to pay by £750.

Task 8

Box 1	Kara Allen
Box 3	15000.00 (2,000 + 13,000)
Box 6	500.00
Box 7	3500.00
Box 10	4200.00
Box 18	1
Box 19	10000.00
Box 20	8000.00
Box 21	2000.00
Box 24	1
Box 25	15500.00
Box 26	16000.00
Box 27	0
Box 30	1
Box 31	17000.00
Box 32	4000.00
Box 33	13000.00

Task 9

(a)

Disposal	Market value used	Actual proceeds used	No gain/no loss disposal
Olivia sells shares for £5,000 to her wife Lucy when they are worth £4,000			✓
William sells land to his brother for £10,000 when it is worth £50,000	✓		
Zeta gives an asset worth £4,000 to her friend Tanya	✓		
Olwyn sells listed shares for proceeds of £12,000		✓	

(b)

The chargeable gain on sale is:

£ 11,150

	£
Proceeds of sale	45,000
Less disposal costs £(900 + 350)	(1,250)
Net proceeds of sale	43,750
Less costs of acquisition £(32,000 + 600)	(32,600)
enhancement expenditure (not reflected in value of property on disposal)	(nil)
Chargeable gain	11,150

(c)

(1) The allowable loss on sale is:

	✓
£3,750	✓
£3,500	
£7,000	
£7,250	

	£
Deemed proceeds of sale	6,000
Less disposal costs (10% × £2,500)	(250)
Net proceeds of sale	5,750
Less cost	(9,500)
Allowable loss	(3,750)

(2) True ☐

False ✓

A chattel with a useful life of 50 years or less is a wasting chattel.

Task 10

Share pool

	No of shares	Cost £
14.4.00 Acquisition	6,000	18,400
29.5.05 Rights 1 for 20 @ £4 (1/20 × 6,000)	300	1,200
	6,300	19,600
23.2.15 Disposal (3,500/6,300 × £19,600)	(3,500)	(10,889)
c/f	2,800	8,711

First match with acquisitions in the next 30 days:

	£
Proceeds of sale $\frac{500}{4,000}$ × £36,200	4,525
Less allowable cost	(3,400)
Gain	1,125
Next match with shares in the share pool	
Proceeds of sale $\frac{3,500}{4,000}$ × £36,200	31,675
Less allowable cost (from share pool above)	(10,889)
Gain	20,786
Total gains (£1,125 + £20,786)	21,911

Task 11

(1)

Explanation	Exempt	Chargeable
Actual occupation	1 April 2000 to 30 September 2003	
Four years employed elsewhere in UK	1 October 2003 to 30 September 2007	
Up to three years any reason	1 October 2007 to 30 September 2008	
Actual occupation	1 October 2008 to 30 April 2009	
Not occupied and not followed by actual occupation		1 May 2009 to 31 March 2013
Last 18 months ownership	1 April 2013 to 30 September 2014	

(2)

After applying principle private residence relief, the sale of Desmond's house will result in a chargeable gain.

True ✓

False ☐

(3)

Capital gains tax for 2014/15 is payable by:

31/01/2016

BPP practice assessment 3: answers

BPP PRACTICE ASSESSMENT 4
PERSONAL TAX

Time allowed: 2 hours

Personal Tax BPP practice assessment 4

TAXATION DATA

Taxation tables for personal tax – 2014/15

Note that 'TAXATION DATA 1' and 'TAXATION DATA 2' shown below will be available as pop up windows throughout your live assessment.

TAXATION DATA 1
Pop-up 1

Tax rates and bands

	%	£
Basic rate	20	first 31,865
Higher rate	40	to 150,000
Additional rate	45	over 150,000

Savings income is taxed at 10%, 20%, 40% and 45%
(10% applies to a maximum of £2,880 of savings income only where non-savings income is below this limit.)

Dividends are taxed at 10%, 32.5% and 37.5%.

Personal allowances

	£
Personal allowance for individuals born after 5 April 1948	10,000
Age allowance for individuals born between 6 April 1938 and 5 April 1948	10,500
Age allowance for individuals born before 6 April 1938	10,660
Income limit for age allowance	27,000

TAXATION DATA 2
Pop-up 2

Car benefit percentage

Emission rating for petrol engines	%
0g/km	0
1g/km to 75g/km	5
76g/km to 94g/km	11
95g/km or more	12% + 1% for every extra 5g/km above 95g/km

Diesel engines – additional 3%

The figure for fuel is £21,700

Authorised mileage rates

First 10,000 miles	45p
Over 10,000 miles	25p

Van scale charge

	£
Charge	3,090
Private fuel provided	581

HMRC official rate   3.25%

Capital gains tax

Annual exempt amount	£11,000
Tax rate	18%
Higher rate	28%

Task 1

Her employer provided Antonia with a secondhand Ford Escort car in October 2013. It cost the company £14,000, but the list price of this car when bought new was £21,000. The car has a CO_2 emission of 90g/km, and has a petrol engine. The company sold the Ford Escort on 31 December 2014 and immediately provided Antonia with a brand new Volvo car. The Volvo has a list price of £27,000, but Antonia had to make a capital contribution of £6,500 towards it. The car has a CO_2 emission of 190g/km and has a diesel engine.

The company pays for all running costs for both cars including the fuel. Antonia pays £80 per month to the company as part of the cost of fuel used privately.

(1) The cost of the Ford Escort in the taxable benefit computation is:

£ ____

(2) The taxable benefit in respect of the provision of the Ford Escort for private use in 2014/15 is:

£ ____

(3) The taxable benefit in respect of the provision of fuel for the Ford Escort for private use in 2014/15 is:

£ ____

(4) The cost of the Volvo in the taxable benefit computation is:

£ ____

(5) The taxable benefit in respect of the provision of the Volvo for private use in 2014/15 is:

£ ____

(6) The taxable benefit in respect of the provision of fuel for the Volvo for private use in 2014/15 is:

£ ____

Task 2

(a)

Elizabeth's employer provided her with a television for her private use on 6 April 2014, costing £2,500. Elizabeth did not pay anything for the use of the TV.

(1) The taxable benefit for 2014/15 is:

£ _____

Elizabeth buys the TV from her employer for £750 on 5 April 2015, when it is worth £1,875.

(2) The taxable benefit for 2014/15 is:

£ _____

(b)

Indicate whether the following benefits would be taxable or exempt if provided in 2014/15, by ticking the boxes:

Item	Taxable	Exempt
Provision of second mobile phone	☐	☐
Removal costs of £7,500	☐	☐
Provision of parking space at work	☐	☐
Accommodation provided to a caretaker for proper performance of his employment duties	☐	☐
Membership of fitness club	☐	☐

Task 3

(a)

Is the following statement True or false?

Property income for a tax year is calculated by taking rental income accrued in the tax year less expenses paid in the tax year.

True ☐

False ☐

(b)

Zhu Liu bought an apartment in October 2014. He let it out, unfurnished, from 1 December 2014 at an annual rent of £18,000 payable quarterly in advance. He incurred the following expenses in relation to the property:

	£
General repairs and maintenance, all incurred prior to 5 April 2015	750
Insurance for the 12 month period ended 30 September 2015	300
Decorating paid for on 31 March 2015, for work carried out on 10 April 2015	500
Installing a shower	1,500

Using the proforma layout provided, calculate the property income for 2014/15. Fill in all the unshaded boxes. If an expense is not allowable, enter 0. Both brackets and minus signs can be used to show negative numbers.

	£
Rental income	
Repairs	
Insurance	
Decorating	
Shower	
Property income	

(c)

Hero lets out a room in her main residence throughout 2014/15. The tenant pays her £50 per week. Hero estimates that she incurs extra costs of £9 per week in relation to the letting. Hero has not made any elections in relation to the letting.

Hero's taxable property income profit/(loss) for 2014/15 is:

	✓
£2,132	
£0	
£(468)	
£(1,650)	

Task 4

(a)

Using the proforma layout provided, show whether the following amounts of interest are received net of basic rate tax or gross by an individual taxpayer:

NS&I Direct Saver Account
Bank interest
NS&I Investment Account
Loan stock from company

Received net	Received gross

(b)

Myrtle was born in 1923, and has the following income for 2014/15: pension income of £18,000, bank interest of £4,800 and dividends of £3,600.

(1) **Myrtle's net income for 2014/15 is:**

£ ☐

(2) **The age allowance that Myrtle is entitled to for 2014/15 is:**

£ ☐

Task 5

(a)

Millie is employed by RST plc. For each of the following payments, state the amount of employment income taxable in 2014/15. If an amount is not taxable in 2014/15 enter 0.

(1) Monthly salary of £2,000. Millie becomes entitled to each month's salary on the 25th of each month and it is paid to her on the 28th of each month. Due to a bank error, the salary for March 2014 was not paid to her until 10 April 2014.

The employment income for 2014/15 is:

£ ☐

(2) Commission of £1,200 paid with her April 2015 salary. The commission relates to sales made in the month of March 2015.

The employment income for 2014/15 is:

£ [ ]

(3) Bonus of £5,000 paid on 30 April 2014 based on company's accounting profit for the year ended 31 December 2013.

The employment income for 2014/15 is:

£ [ ]

(4) Reimbursement of business expenses of £500 in December 2013. There is a dispensation in force for such payments with HMRC.

The employment income for 2014/15 is:

£ [ ]

(b)
In 2014/15, Calum had the following income:

Salary £47,300
Building society interest £144
Dividends £90

Calum made a contribution of £2,500 to his employer's occupational pension scheme.

Using the proforma layout provided, prepare a computation of taxable income for 2014/15, clearly showing the distinction between the different types of income. Both brackets and minus signs can be used to show negative numbers.

	Non-savings income £	Savings income £	Dividend income £	Total £

Task 6

(a)

Ian had has the following amounts of taxable income (AFTER deduction of his personal allowance) for 2014/15:

	£
Non-savings income	38,382
Savings income	180
Dividend income	400

Ian paid £100 to Oxfam in November 2014 and made a Gift Aid declaration.

Ian's tax liability on each source of income for 2014/15 is as follows:

(1) **Non-savings income:**

£ ☐

(2) **Savings income:**

£ ☐

(3) **Dividend income:**

£ ☐

(b)

(1)

Max earns £2,500 in 2014/15 in a part-time job. He also has property income of £15,000 in 2014/15 from letting out a field.

The maximum personal pension contribution on which Max can get tax relief in 2014/15 is:

	✓
£2,500	
£3,600	
£7,500	
£5,000	

(2)

Max's tax liability for 2014/15 is:

£ ☐

Task 7

(a)

A client has told you that she forgot to include some bank interest in the tax return you prepared and she does not intend to tell HMRC of the omission.

What TWO actions should you take?

	✓
Inform the Association of Accounting Technicians about the omission	
Report the client's refusal and the facts surrounding it to your firm's Money Laundering Reporting Officer	
Inform the client in writing that it is not possible for you to act for her in connection with that return	
Inform HMRC about the omission	

(b)

> 1 Horse Lane
> Trotter Village
> Westhampton
> WW44 1EE
>
> 28 November 2015
>
> Dear Accountant
>
> Please find enclosed all the information that I think you will need to complete my tax return for 2014/15.
>
> However, I have never had to complete a tax return before, and as the tax year ended some months ago, I am a little concerned that I may have missed a crucial deadline.
>
> Please advise me when my return is due and if I will incur any penalties. Also I would like to know when I need to pay any tax that I owe.
>
> Regards
>
> Mahmood

Write notes for inclusion in your reply to Mahmood's letter.

Task 8

You act for Saul Bentner. He owns two properties and has given you the following information:

	Property A	Property B
	£	£
Annual income:		
Rent	6,000	4,000
Annual expenses:		
Redecoration	1,000	800
Cleaning	300	n/a
Insurance	350	250
Letting agent's fees	1,500	400

Property A is let furnished. Property B is let unfurnished.

Using this information complete the property income pages of Saul's tax return.

UK property
Tax year 6 April 2014 to 5 April 2015

HM Revenue & Customs

Your name

Your Unique Taxpayer Reference (UTR)

UK property details

1. Number of properties rented out

2. If all property income ceased in 2014–15 and you do not expect to receive such income in 2015–16, put 'X' in the box and consider if you need to complete the *Capital gains summary* page

3. If you have any income from property let jointly, put 'X' in the box

4. If you are claiming Rent a Room relief and your rents are £4,250 or less nor £2,125 if let jointly), put 'X' in the box

Furnished holiday lettings (FHL) in the UK or European Economic Area (EEA)

Fill in one page for UK businesses and a separate page for EEA businesses. Please read the *UK property notes* before filling in boxes 5 to 19 if you have furnished holiday lettings

5. **Income** – *the amount of rent and any income for services provided to tenants*
   £

6. **Rent paid, repairs, insurance and costs of services provided** – *the total amount*
   £

7. **Loan interest and other financial cost**
   £

8. **Legal, management and other professional fee**
   £

9. **Other allowable property expenses**
   £

10. **Private use adjustment** – *if expenses include any amounts for non-business purposes*
    £

11. **Balancing charges** – *read the notes*
    £

12. **Capital allowances** – *read the notes*
    £

13. **Adjusted profit for the year** (if the amount in box 5 + box 10 + box 11 minus (boxes 6 to 9 + box 12) is positive)
    £

14. **Loss brought forward used against this year's profit** – *if you have a non-FHL property business loss read the notes on property losses*
    £

15. **Taxable profit for the year** (box 13 minus box 14)
    £

16. **Loss for the year** (if the amount in boxes 6 to 9 + box 12 minus (box 5 + box 10 + box 11) is positive)
    £

17. **Total loss to carry forward**
    £

18. If this business is in the EEA, put 'X' in the box – *read the notes*

19. If you want to make a period of grace election, put 'X' in the box

SA105 2014   Page UKP 1   HMRC 12/14

BPP practice assessment 4: questions

Property income

Do not include furnished holiday lettings, Real Estate Investment Trust or Property Authorised Investment Funds dividends/distributions here.

20 Total rents and other income from property
£ _____ . 0 0

21 Tax taken off any income in box 20
£ _____ . 0 0

22 Premiums for the grant of a lease – from box E on the Working Sheet – *read the notes*
£ _____ . 0 0

23 Reverse premiums and inducements
£ _____ . 0 0

Property expenses

24 Rent, rates, insurance, ground rents etc
£ _____ . 0 0

25 Property repairs, maintenance and renewals
£ _____ . 0 0

26 Loan interest and other financial cost
£ _____ . 0 0

27 Legal, management and other professional fee
£ _____ . 0 0

28 Costs of services provided, including wages
£ _____ . 0 0

29 Other allowable property expenses
£ _____ . 0 0

Calculating your taxable profit or loss

30 Private use adjustment – *read the notes*
£ _____ . 0 0

31 Balancing charges – *read the notes*
£ _____ . 0 0

32 Annual Investment Allowance
£ _____ . 0 0

33 Business Premises Renovation Allowance (Assisted Areas only) – *read the notes*
£ _____ . 0 0

34 All other capital allowances
£ _____ . 0 0

35 Landlord's Energy Saving Allowance
£ _____ . 0 0

36 10% wear and tear allowance – *for furnished residential accommodation only*
£ _____ . 0 0

37 Rent a Room exempt amount
£ _____ . 0 0

38 Adjusted profit for the year – from box O on the Working Sheet – *read the notes*
£ _____ . 0 0

39 Loss brought forward used against this year's profit
£ _____ . 0 0

40 Taxable profit for the year (box 38 minus box 39)
£ _____ . 0 0

41 Adjusted loss for the year – from box O on the Working Sheet – *read the notes*
£ _____ . 0 0

42 Loss set off against 2014–15 total income – *this will be unusual – read the notes*
£ _____ . 0 0

43 Loss to carry forward to following year, including unused losses brought forward
£ _____ . 0 0

Sa105 2014　　　　　　　　　Page UKP 2

Task 9

(a)

Classify whether a disposal of each of the following assets will be chargeable to or exempt from capital gains tax:

Asset	Chargeable	Exempt
Plot of land sold for £20,000	☐	☐
Diamond brooch sold for £3,500 which cost £2,000	☐	☐
Shares in an unlisted company sold for £10,000	☐	☐
1930 Rolls Royce car sold for £100,000	☐	☐

(b)

Jaycee made the following gains and loss in 2014/15:

	£
Gain on shares September 2014	18,400
Gain on painting December 2014	6,000
Gain on house January 2015 (not her PPR)	18,895
Loss on vase April 2014	(10,000)

Jaycee is a higher rate taxpayer.

(1) **Her capital gains tax liability for 2014/15 is:**

£ ☐

(2) **The due date for payment of this liability is:** (enter date as xx/xx/xxxx)

☐

(c)

In December 2014, Mabel gave her son an asset worth £20,000. She had acquired the asset for £25,000.

In March 2015, Mabel gave her sister an asset worth £30,000. Mable had acquired the asset for £22,000.

Mabel's chargeable gains (before the annual exempt amount) for 2014/15 are:

£ ☐

Task 10

Ming Lee bought 1,000 shares in Lavender Ltd for £5,000 in October 2004. In May 2006, she received 200 shares in a bonus issue. In January 2010 the company offered a rights issue at 1 share for every 6 held. She accepted this rights issue at £3 per share. She sold 1,000 shares in Lavender Ltd in January 2015 for £12,400.

Clearly showing the balance of shares and their value to carry forward, calculate the chargeable gain on sale of the shares. All workings must be shown.

Task 11

(a)

On 1 March 1994, Craig bought a house for £36,000. He had lived in it until 1 September 1997, when he went to Australia to take up employment. He returned from there on 1 September 2003 and moved back into the house until 1 February 2009 when he purchased a small flat. He has lived in the flat since then. Craig finally sold the house for £178,000 on 31 October 2014.

Using the proforma layout below, show the chargeable gain on sale. Both brackets and minus signs can be used to show negative numbers.

Chargeable gain on sale of property	£
Proceeds of sale	
Less allowable cost	
Gain before PPR	
Less PPR exempt amount	
Chargeable gain	

(b)

During 2014/15 Nina has sold an asset giving rise to a chargeable gain of £20,000. She has capital losses brought forward at 6 April 2014 of £11,000.

The amount of capital losses Nina will have to carry forward at 5 April 2015 is

	✓
£2,000	
£0	
£11,000	
£9,000	

BPP PRACTICE ASSESSMENT 4
PERSONAL TAX

ANSWERS

BPP practice assessment 4: answers

Personal Tax BPP practice assessment 4

Task 1

(1) The cost of the Ford Escort in the taxable benefit computation is:

£ 21,000

(2) The taxable benefit in respect of the provision of the Ford Escort for private use in 2014/15 is:

£ 1,733   £21,000 × 11% (CO_2 emissions of 90g/km) × 9/12

(3) The taxable benefit in respect of the provision of fuel for the Ford Escort for private use in 2014/15 is:

£ 1,790

£21,700 × 11% × 9/12 (no reduction for partial reimbursement of private fuel)

(4) The cost of the Volvo in the taxable benefit computation is:

£ 22,000   £27,000 – £5,000 (max deduction for capital contribution)

(5) The taxable benefit in respect of the provision of the Volvo for private use in 2014/15 is:

£ 1,870   £22,000 × 34% × 3/12

190 – 95 = 95

95 ÷ 5 = 19%

12% + 19% + 3% (diesel) = 34%

(6) The taxable benefit in respect of the provision of fuel for the Volvo for private use in 2014/15 is:

£ 1,845

£21,700 × 34% × 3/12 (no reduction for partial reimbursement of private fuel)

BPP practice assessment 4: answers

Task 2

(a)

(1) The taxable benefit for 2014/15 is:

£ | 500

Use of asset £2,500 × 20%

(2) The taxable benefit for 2014/15 is:

£ | 1,250

		£
Greater of:		
(i) Original market value		2,500
Less assessed for use 2014/15		(500)
		2,000
(ii) Market rate at acquisition by employee		1,875

Greater = £2,000 less amount paid by Elizabeth of £750

(b)

Item	Taxable	Exempt
Provision of second mobile phone	✓	
Removal costs of £7,500		✓
Provision of parking space at work		✓
Accommodation provided to a caretaker for proper performance of his employment duties		✓
Membership of fitness club	✓	

Task 3

(a)

True ☐

False ✓

Property income for a tax year is calculated by taking rental income accrued in the tax year less expenses accrued in the tax year.

(b)

	£
Rental income £18,000 × 4/12	6,000
Repairs	(750)
Insurance £300 × 6/12	(150)
Decorating (not accrued in 2014/15)	0
Shower (capital expense)	0
Property income	5,100

(c)
Hero's taxable property income profit/(loss) for 2014/15 is

	✓
£2,132	
£0	✓
£(468)	
£(1,650)	

Hero has no taxable property income profit for 2014/15 because the income from the letting is £50 × 52 = £2,600, which is less than the rent a room limit. Rent a room relief applies automatically when rental income is below £4,250, unless the taxpayer makes an election to use the usual property income rules.

Task 4

(a)

Received net	Received gross
Bank interest	NS&I Direct Saver Account
Loan stock from company	NS&I Investment Account

BPP practice assessment 4: answers

(b)

(1) Myrtle's net income for 2014/15 is:

£ 28,000

	Non-savings income £	Savings income £	Dividend income £	Total £
Pension income	18,000			
Bank interest (× 100/80)		6,000		
Dividends (× 100/90)			4,000	
Net income	18,000	6,000	4,000	28,000

(2) The age allowance that Myrtle is entitled to for 2014/15 is:

£ 10,160

	£
Total net income	28,000
Less income limit	(27,000)
Excess	1,000
Age allowance	10,660
Less half excess	(500)
	10,160

....

Task 5

(a)

(1) The employment income for 2014/15 is:

£ 24,000

April 2014 to March 2015 = 12 × £2,000

The salary for March 2014 was received for tax purposes on 25 March 2014 when Millie became entitled to it and so was taxed in 2013/14.

278

(2) The employment income for 2014/15 is:

£ | 0

Commission received 25 April 2015 (taxed in 2015/16)

(3) The employment income for 2014/15 is:

£ | 5,000

Bonus received 30 April 2014

(4) The employment income for 2014/15 is:

£ | 0

Reimbursement with dispensation (ignored)

(b)

	Non-savings income £	Savings income £	Dividend income £	Total £
Employment income:				
Salary	47,300			
Less occupational pension contribution	(2,500)			
Employment income	44,800			
Building society interest (× 100/80)		180		
Dividends (× 100/90)			100	
Net income	44,800	180	100	45,080
Less personal allowance	(10,000)			(10,000)
Taxable income	34,800	180	100	35,080

Task 6

(a)

(1) Non-savings income:

| £ | 8,955 |

	£
£31,865 × 20%	6,373
£125 (£100 × 100/80) × 20% (extended band)	25
£6,392 × 40%	2,557
	8,955

(2) Savings income:

| £ | 72 |

£180 × 40%

(3) Dividend income:

| £ | 130 |

£400 × 32.5%

(b)

(1)

The maximum pension contribution on which Max can get tax relief in 2014/15 is:

£2,500	
£3,600	✓
£7,500	
£5,000	

Higher of earnings and £3,600. Property income is not earnings unless it is from qualifying holiday accommodation.

(2) Max's tax liability for 2014/15 is:

| £ | 1,500 |

£2,500 + £15,000 = £17,500

Less PA of £10,000 = £7,500 (Taxable non-savings income)
£7,500 × 20%   1,500

Task 7

(a)

	✓
Inform the Association of Accounting Technicians about the omission	
Report the client's refusal and the facts surrounding it to your firm's Money Laundering Reporting Officer	✓
Inform the client in writing that it is not possible for you to act for her in connection with that return	✓
Inform HMRC about the omission	

(b)

There are two key dates for when tax returns are due:

For paper based version of the tax return it is 31 October 2015 (now passed)

For electronic based version of the tax return it is 31 January 2016

Provided that the return is completed by 31 January 2016 no penalty will be payable. The tax liability will automatically be calculated on completion of the online return.

If you owe any tax this will be due on the same date. Also you may then need to make interim payments for 2015/16. The first of these will also be due on 31 January 2016 and will be calculated as half of the amount of tax due by self assessment for 2014/15.

Task 8

Your name:	Saul Bentner
Box 1	2
Box 20	10000.00
Box 24	600.00
Box 25	1800.00
Box 27	1900.00
Box 28	300.00
Box 36	600.00
Box 38	4800.00
Box 40	4800.00

Task 9

(a)

Asset	Chargeable	Exempt
Plot of land sold for £20,000	✓	
Diamond brooch sold for £3,500 which cost £2,000		✓ (cost and proceeds no more than £6,000)
Shares in an unlisted company sold for £10,000	✓	
1930 Rolls Royce car sold for £100,000		✓ (all cars exempt)

(b)

(1) Her capital gains tax liability for 2014/15 is:

£ 6,243

	£
Gain on shares	18,400
Gain on painting	6,000
Gain on house	18,895
Chargeable gains	43,295
Less allowable loss on vase	(10,000)
Net chargeable gains for year	33,295
Less annual exempt amount	(11,000)
Taxable gains	22,295
CGT @ 28%	6,243

(2) The due date for payment of this liability is:

31/01/2016

(c)

Mabel's chargeable gains (before the annual exempt amount) for 2014/15 are:

£ 8,000

	£
Gift to her sister:	
Deemed proceeds of sale (market value)	30,000
Less allowable cost	(22,000)
Chargeable gain	8,000

Both the son and the sister are connected persons for Mabel. However, the loss on the disposal to the son of £5,000 can only be set against gains made to him, not to another connected person.

Task 10

Share pool

	No of shares	Cost £
October 2004 Acquisition	1,000	5,000
May 2006 Bonus	200	nil
	1,200	5,000
January 2010 Rights 1 for 6 @ £3	200	600
(1/6 × 1,200 = 200 shares @ £3 = £600)		
	1,400	5,600
January 2015 Disposal		
(1,000/1,400 × £5,600)	(1,000)	(4,000)
c/f	400	1,600

Gain

	£
Proceeds of sale	12,400
Less allowable cost	(4,000)
Chargeable gain	8,400

Task 11

(a)

Chargeable gain on sale of property	£
Proceeds of sale	178,000
Less allowable cost	(36,000)
Gain before PPR	142,000
Less PPR exempt amount (W) £142,000 × 197/248	(112,798)
Chargeable gain	29,202

Working

Time period	Chargeable months	Exempt months	Total months
1.3.94 to 31.8.97		42	42
1.9.97 to 31.8.03 (Note 1)		72	72
1.9.03 to 31.1.09		65	65
1.2.09 to 31.10.14 (Note 2)	51	18	69
	51	197	248

Notes

1. Any period of employment abroad is treated as deemed occupation if it is preceded and followed by actual occupation.

2. Last 18 months of ownership is always exempt if the property has been the taxpayer's only or main residence at some time during the ownership period.

(b)

The amount of capital losses Nina will have to carry forward at 5 April 2015 is

	✓
£2,000	✓
£0	
£11,000	
£9,000	

The capital loss brought forward will be used to bring the chargeable gain for 2014/15 to the level of the annual exempt amount. This uses £9,000 of the loss leaving £2,000 to carry forward to 2015/16.

BPP PRACTICE ASSESSMENT 5
PERSONAL TAX

Time allowed: 2 hours

Personal Tax BPP practice assessment 5

TAXATION DATA

Taxation tables for personal tax – 2014/15

Note that 'TAXATION DATA 1' and 'TAXATION DATA 2' shown below will be available as pop-up windows throughout your live assessment.

TAXATION DATA 1
Pop-up 1

Tax rates and bands

	%	£
Basic rate	20	first 31,865
Higher rate	40	to 150,000
Additional rate	45	over 150,000

Savings income is taxed at 10%, 20%, 40% and 45%
(10% applies to a maximum of £2,880 of savings income only where non-savings income is below this limit.)

Dividends are taxed at 10%, 32.5% and 37.5%.

Personal allowances

	£
Personal allowance for individuals born after 5 April 1948	10,000
Age allowance for individuals born between 6 April 1938 and 5 April 1948	10,500
Age allowance for individuals born before 6 April 1938	10,660
Income limit for age allowance	27,000

TAXATION DATA 2

Car benefit percentage

Emission rating for petrol engines	%
0g/km	0
1g/km to 75g/km	5
76g/km to 94g/km	11
95g/km or more	12% + 1% for every extra 5g/km above 95g/km

Diesel engines – additional 3%

The figure for fuel is £21,700

Authorised mileage rates

First 10,000 miles	45p
Over 10,000 miles	25p

Van scale charge

	£
Charge	3,090
Private fuel provided	581

HMRC official rate   3.25%

Capital gains tax

Annual exempt amount	£11,000
Tax rate	18%
Higher rate	28%

Task 1

(a)

Yan is provided with a company car for business and private use throughout 2014/15. The car had a list price of £17,200 when bought new in December 2013, although the company paid £16,000 for the car after a dealer discount. Yan made a contribution of £2,000 to the cost of the car.

The car has a petrol engine and has CO_2 emissions of 127g/km. The company pays for all running costs, including all fuel. Yan does not make any contribution for his private use of the car.

(1) The cost of the car in the taxable benefit computation is:

£ [ ]

(2) The percentage used in the taxable benefit computation is:

[ ] %

(3) The taxable benefit in respect of the provision of fuel for private use is:

£ [ ]

(b)

You have received the following email from Matt Taylor:

From:	MTaylor@boxmail.net
To:	AATStudent@boxmail.net
Sent:	14 June 2015 11:35
Subject:	Car

I have recently been promoted and now have to do some travelling by car on business, probably about 6,000 miles a year. My employer has given me two options:

(1) A company car with a list price of £15,000. It has a petrol engine. The car is environmentally friendly and so has CO_2 emissions of only 85g/km. I will be able to use the car for both business and private purposes, but I will be required to repay the cost of my private fuel.

(2) A mileage allowance of 35p per business mile if I use my own car.

Can you please explain the taxation aspects of each of the options?

Thanks, Matt

Reply to Matt's email.

Task 2

(a)

(1) Marge has recently started to work for LMN plc and earns £30,000 a year. She is entitled to childcare vouchers of £60 per week for 45 weeks in 2014/15.

The taxable benefit for 2014/15 is:

£ [ ]

(2) **Tick to show if the following statement is True or False.**

The maximum amount of exempt benefit for the additional costs of home working is £4 per week.

True [ ]

False [ ]

(b)

For each of the following benefits, tick whether they would be wholly or partly taxable or wholly exempt if received in 2014/15:

Item	Wholly or partly taxable	Wholly exempt
Award of £25 under staff suggestion scheme	[ ]	[ ]
Removal expenses of £9,000	[ ]	[ ]
Incidental personal expenses of working away from home in the UK of £10 per night	[ ]	[ ]
Staff party at cost of £100 per head	[ ]	[ ]

(c)

Antonia is employed by Zed Ltd. She receives store vouchers from the company as a Christmas bonus in December 2014. These enable her to buy goods worth £300. Her employer bought the vouchers from the store for £267.

(1) **The taxable benefit for 2014/15 is:**

£ [ ]

Antonia is also made a loan of £12,000 by Zed Ltd on 1 July 2014. She pays interest at an annual rate of 0.5% on the loan. She does not make any capital repayments in 2014/15.

(2) **The taxable benefit for 2014/15 is:**

£ [ ]

Task 3

(a)

Ronnie buys a house on 6 May 2014 and rents it out on 6 August 2014. He charges an annual rent of £9,000, payable in advance. He pays an annual insurance premium on 6 June 2014 of £600.

Ronnie's taxable property income for 2014/15 is:

£ [   ]

(b)

A client, Mohamed Albayouk, has sent in the following information for 2014/15 in relation to his two properties that he rents out.

17 Wool Lane is unfurnished and is rented out at £560 per month. 42 Silk Street is furnished and is rented out at £800 per month. Both properties were fully occupied during 2014/15.

The expenses for the year were:

Item	17 Wool Lane £	42 Silk Street £
Insurance	300	280
Water rates	160	176
Council tax	1,800	2,100
Cleaning	800	500
Redecoration	1,000	0
Cost of furniture	0	3,450

The wear and tear allowance is claimed where relevant.

Calculate the property income taxable on Mohamed Albayouk for 2014/15 using the proforma layout provided. Fill in all the unshaded boxes. If any item is not an allowable expense, enter 0. Both brackets and minus signs can be used to show negative numbers.

	17 Wool Lane	42 Silk Street
	£	£
Income:		
Rents		
Expenses:		
Insurance		
Water rates		
Council tax		
Cleaning		
Redecoration		
Furniture		
Wear and tear		
Property income		
Total Property income		

(c)

Asif owns three properties which he lets out throughout 2014/15. He makes a profit of £5,000 on Property 1, a loss of £1,200 on Property 2 and a profit of £2,000 on Property 3. Asif also has a property loss of £1,500 brought forward at 5 April 2014.

The property income taxable on Asif for 2014/15 is:

£ ☐

Task 4

(a)

During 2014/15, Mimi received the following income. In each case, show the amount of income that she should enter on her tax return. If the income is exempt, enter 0.

(1) Property income £2,000.

£ ☐

(2) Premium bond prize £100.

£ ☐

(3) NS&I Direct Saver account interest £80.

£ ☐

(4) Dividends received £1,800.

£ ☐

(b)

Marcello receives a dividend of £5,400 in March 2015.

(1) **The amount of the dividend that Marcello will enter on his tax return is:**

£ ☐

(2) **The tax credit attaching to the dividend is:**

£ ☐

(3) Marcello has no other income.

Is the following statement True or False?

Marcello will receive a repayment of the amount of the tax credit.

True ☐

False ☐

Task 5

Andrea is a director of Z Ltd and provides you with the following information:

(1) Monthly salary of £7,500 paid on 25th day of each month

(2) Bonus A of £17,500 based on company's accounting profit for the period of account ended 31 March 2014, determined on 31 October 2014. Andrea became entitled to be paid this bonus on 30 April 2015 and it was actually paid to her on 30 June 2015.

(3) Bonus B of £22,500 based on company's accounting profit for the period of account ended 31 July 2015, determined on 31 March 2015. Andrea became entitled to be paid this bonus on 30 June 2015 and it was actually paid to her on 30 September 2015.

(4) 5% of basic salary paid into the company pension scheme each tax year, Z Ltd matches these contributions.

(5) Use of a company car which has a taxable benefit for 2014/15 of £3,250. No fuel is provided for private use.

(6) Dividends received of £3,800, and interest of £750 from a new ISA.

BPP practice assessment 5: questions

Complete the following table showing the figures to be included in Andrea's taxable income for 2014/15. Use whole pounds only. If your answer is zero, please insert a '0'. Do not use brackets or minus signs.

	£
Salary	
Bonus A	
Bonus B	
Director's pension contribution	
Company's pension contribution	
Company car benefit	
Dividends	
Interest from NISA	
Net income	
Personal allowance	
Taxable income	

Task 6

Andrew, born in 1966, has income as follows:

	£
Employment income	46,000
Bank interest received	1,600
Dividends received	4,500

Andrew makes a Gift Aid donation of £1,200 in July 2014.

(a)

Calculate his total income tax liability for 2014/15, using the table given below. Both brackets and minus signs can be used to show negative numbers.

	£

(b)

On which dates are payment on accounts due for 2014/15?

	✓
31 January 2015 and 31 July 2015	
31 January 2016 and 31 July 2016	
31 July 2015 and 31 January 2016	
31 October 2015 and 31 January 2016	

Task 7

(a)

You are a sole practitioner and suspect that one of your clients may be engaged in money laundering.

Who should you inform about your suspicions?

	✓
Serious Organised Crime Agency	
Association of Taxation Technicians	
Tax Tribunal	
HM Treasury	

(b)

On 30 September 2015 your client, Jakki, leaves the following message on your voicemail:

> 'Hi, it's Jakki. I know that I am a new client to your practice and that you did not prepare my tax return for 2013/14, but I have just discovered that I failed to notify HMRC of some dividends that I received in January 2014. I simply forgot about them, but I am worried that HMRC will find out that I have not paid the right amount of tax on this income. Can you please advise about what I should do and about any penalties that I may incur? Thanks.'

List the information that you need to give Jakki when you ring her back to discuss this issue.

Task 8

You act for Gary Bryant, who works for HGK plc. He has given you the following information about his employment in relation to the tax year 2014/15:

	£
Gross salary	30,000
Occupational pension payment deducted	2,500
Tax taken off pay	4,200
Company car benefit	3,200
Private medical insurance	1,500
Professional subscription paid by Gary	300

Using this information complete the employment income page.

HM Revenue & Customs

Employment
Tax year 6 April 2014 to 5 April 2015

Your name

Your unique taxpayer reference (UTR)

Complete an *Employment* page for each employment or directorship

1 Pay from this employment - the total from your P45 or P60 - *before tax was taken off*

£

2 UK tax taken off pay in box 1

£

3 Tips and other payments not on your P60 - *read page EN 3 of the notes*

£

4 PAYE tax reference of your employer (on your P45/P60)

5 Your employer's name

6 If you were a company director, put 'X' in the box

7 And, if the company was a close company, put 'X' in the box

8 If you are a part-time teacher in England or Wales and are on the Repayment of Teachers' Loans Scheme for this employment, put 'X' in the box

Benefits from your employment - use your form P11D (or equivalent information)

9 Company cars and vans - *the total 'cash equivalent' amount*

£

10 Fuel for company cars and vans - *the total 'cash equivalent' amount*

£

11 Private medical and dental insurance - *the total 'cash equivalent' amount*

£

12 Vouchers, credit cards and excess mileage allowance

£

13 Goods and other assets provided by your employer - *the total value or amount*

£

14 Accommodation provided by your employer - *the total value or amount*

£

15 Other benefits (including interest-free and low interest loans) - *the total 'cash equivalent' amount*

£

16 Expenses payments received and balancing charges

£

Employment expenses

17 Business travel and subsistence expenses

£

18 Fixed deductions for expenses

£

19 Professional fees and subscriptions

£

20 Other expenses and capital allowances

£

Shares schemes, employment lump sums, compensation, deductions and Seafarers' Earnings Deduction are on the *Additional information* pages enclosed in the tax return pack

SA102 2014   Tax return: Employment: Page E 1   HMRC 12/13

Task 9

(a)

For each of the following assets, tick whether they are chargeable or exempt assets for capital gains tax:

Asset	Chargeable	Exempt
Horse	☐	☐
Field in which horse is kept	☐	☐
Antique horse brass costing £500, worth £1,700	☐	☐

(b)

Ulma bought a holiday cottage for £65,000 and spent £15,000 on an extension and £10,000 on redecoration. She sold the cottage for £125,000 on 10 August 2014.

The chargeable gain on sale is:

£ ☐

(c)

Jade purchased a emerald bracelet for £8,000. She sold the bracelet in August 2014 at auction for £2,700 (which was net of 10% commission).

The allowable loss on sale is:

£ ☐

Task 10

Merrill paid £5,000 for 2,000 shares in Bug plc in August 2008. In September 2011, there was a one for one bonus issue. Merrill sold 1,000 shares in June 2014 for £8,000.

Compute the chargeable gain and the value of the share pool following the disposal, using the proforma layout provided. Both brackets and minus signs can be used to show negative numbers.

Gain

	£

Share pool

	No of shares	Cost £

Task 11

(a)

Jai makes chargeable gains of £15,000 in November 2014. Jai's taxable income for 2014/15 is £31,470 and he made a Gift Aid payment of £400 to Oxfam in May 2014.

The CGT payable for 2014/15 is:

£ ☐

(b)

Tick to show if the following statement is True or False.

The last 18 months of ownership of a house are exempt provided that the house is lived in by the owner at some time during that 18 month period.

True ☐

False ☐

BPP PRACTICE ASSESSMENT 5
PERSONAL TAX

ANSWERS

# Personal Tax BPP practice assessment 5

Task 1

(a)

(1) The cost of the car in the taxable benefit computation is:

| £ | 15,200 |

List price less capital contribution made by Yan

(2) The percentage used in the taxable benefit computation is:

| 18 | % |

125 − 95 = 30

30 ÷ 5 = 6%

12% + 6%

(3) The taxable benefit in respect of the provision of fuel for private use is:

| £ | 3,906 |

£21,700 × 18%

(b)

From:	AAT Student@boxmail.net
To:	MTaylor@boxmail.net
Sent:	16 June 2015 10.41
Subject:	Car

The provision of the company car will be a taxable benefit because it is available for private use. The benefit is the list price of the car multiplied by a percentage. In this case, because the car has CO_2 emissions of between 76g/km and 94g/km, the percentage will be 11%. The benefit will therefore be £15,000 × 11% = £1,650 per tax year. There will be no fuel benefit because you will be reimbursing the cost of your private fuel.

There is a statutory mileage allowance which would apply if you use your own car for business purposes. The rate is 45p per mile up to 10,000 miles per year. As your employer would only be paying you 35p per mile, the extra 10p per mile could be claimed by you as an allowable deduction when working out your employment income. If you travelled 6,000 business miles in a tax year, the deduction would be 6,000 × 10p = £600.

Task 2

(a)

(1) The taxable benefit for 2014/15 is:

£ 225

£(60 − 55) = £5 × 45

(2) True ☐
    False ☑

Payments in excess of £4 per week can be exempt benefits provided that evidence will be given that the payment is wholly in respect of additional household expenses incurred by the employee in carrying out his duties at home.

(b)

Item	Wholly or partly taxable	Wholly exempt
Award of £25 under staff suggestion scheme		✓
Removal expenses of £9,000	✓ (limit £8,000))	
Incidental personal expenses of working away from home in the UK of £10 per night	✓ (wholly taxable if exceeds £5)	
Staff party at cost of £100 per head		✓ (up to £150)

(c)

(1) The taxable benefit for 2014/15 is:

£ 267

Cost to employer

(2) The taxable benefit for 2014/15 is:

£ 248

£12,000 × (3.25 − 0.5)% × 9/12

Task 3

(a)

Ronnie's taxable property income for 2014/15 is:

£ | 5,500

	£
Rent accrued £9,000 × 8/12	6,000
Less expense £600 × 10/12	(500)
Property income 2014/15	5,500

Income and expenses are taxed on the accruals basis.

(b)

	17 Wool Lane £	42 Silk Street £
Income:		
Rents £560/800 × 12	6,720	9,600
Expenses:		
Insurance	(300)	(280)
Water rates	(160)	(176)
Council tax	(1,800)	(2,100)
Cleaning	(800)	(500)
Redecoration	(1,000)	0
Furniture	0	0
Wear and tear £(9,600 – 176 – 2,100) × 10%	0	(732)
Property income	2,660	5,812
Total property income		8,472

(c)

The property income taxable on Asif for 2014/15 is:

£ | 4,300

	£
Property 1 profit	5,000
Property 2 loss	(1,200)
Property 3 profit	2,000
	5,800
Less loss b/f	(1,500)
Property income 2014/15	4,300

Task 4

(a)

(1) Property income £2,000.

| £ | 2,000 |

(2) Premium bond prize £100.

| £ | 0 |

Exempt

(3) NS&I Direct Saver account interest £80.

| £ | 80 |

Received gross

(4) Dividends received £1,800

| £ | 2,000 |

£1,800 × 100/90

(b)

(1) The amount of the dividend that Marcello will enter on his tax return is:

| £ | 6,000 |

£5,400 × 100/90

(2) The tax credit attaching to the dividend is:

| £ | 600 |

£6,000 × 10%

(3) True ☐
    False ☑

The tax credit cannot be repaid.

Task 5

	£
Salary (£7,500 × 12)	90,000
Bonus A (treated as received on 31 October 2014)	17,500
Bonus B (treated as received on 30 June 2015 – taxed 2015/16)	0
Director's pension contribution (£90,000 × 5%)	4,500
Company's pension contribution (non-taxable benefit)	0
Company car benefit	3,250
Dividends (£3,800 × 100/90)	4,222
Interest from NISA	0
Net income	110,472
Personal allowance £(10,000 – ((110,472 – 100,000)/2))	4,764
Taxable income	105,708

Task 6

(a)

	£
Employment income	46,000
Bank interest £1,600 × 100/80	2,000
Dividends £4,500 × 100/90	5,000
	53,000
Personal allowance	(10,000)
Taxable income	43,000

Tax on non-savings income:

£31,865 × 20%	6,373
£1,500 (£1,200 × 100/80) × 20%	300
£2,635 × 40%	1,054

Tax on savings income:

£2,000 × 40%	800

Tax on dividend income:

£5,000 × 32½ %	1,625
Income Tax Liability	10,152

(b)

On which dates are payment on accounts due for 2014/15?

	✓
31 January 2015 and 31 July 2015	✓
31 January 2016 and 31 July 2016	
31 July 2015 and 31 January 2016	
31 October 2015 and 31 January 2016	

Payments on account are due on 31 January in the tax year and 31 July following the end of the tax year.

Task 7

(a)

	✓
Serious Organised Crime Agency	✓
Association of Taxation Technicians	
Tax Tribunal	
HM Treasury	

(b)

Incorrect tax return

The maximum penalty for a careless (rather than a deliberate) error is 30% of the potential lost revenue (ie tax lost). Obviously this is only relevant if Jakki is a higher rate taxpayer, as the tax credit attaching to the dividend would cover her basic rate liability.

However, any penalty may be reduced to 0% if Jakki makes an unprompted disclosure. An unprompted disclosure is one made at a time when the taxpayer has no reason to believe HMRC has discovered, or is about to discover, the error. Jakki should therefore make disclosure to HMRC as soon as possible.

Task 8

Name	Gary Bryant
Box 1	27500.00
Box 2	4200.00
Box 5	HGK plc
Box 9	3200.00
Box 11	1500.00
Box 19	300.00

Task 9

(a)

Asset	Chargeable	Exempt
Horse		✓ (wasting asset)
Field in which horse is kept	✓	
Antique horse brass costing £500, worth £1,700		✓ (exempt chattel)

(b)

The chargeable gain on sale is:

£ 45,000

	£
Proceeds of sale	125,000
Less cost	(65,000)
enhancement expenditure	(15,000)
Chargeable gain	45,000

(c)

The allowable loss on sale is:

£ 2,300

	£
Deemed disposal proceeds	6,000
Less disposal costs £(2,700 × 100/90) × 10%	(300)
Net proceeds	5,700
Less cost	(8,000)
Allowable loss	(2,300)

Task 10

Gain

	£
Proceeds of sale	8,000
Less cost	(1,250)
Chargeable gain	6,750

Share pool

	No of shares	Cost £
August 2008 Acquisition	2,000	5,000
September 2011 Bonus 1 for 1	2,000	0
	4,000	5,000
June 2014 Disposal		
(1,000/4,000 × £5,000)	(1,000)	(1,250)
c/f	3,000	3,750

Task 11

The CGT payable for 2014/15 is:

(a)

£	1,030

	£
Gains	15,000
Less annual exempt amount	(11,000)
Taxable gains	4,000
CGT	
£895 (W) @ 18%	161
£3,105 @ 28%	869
CGT	1,030

(W) Unused basic rate band is £31,865 + £500 (£400 × 100/80) − £31,470 = £895

(b)

True ☐

False ☑

Provided the house has been occupied by the owner as his only or main residence at some time during the period of ownership, the last 18 months of ownership are exempt whether or not the owner lives in the house during that period.

TAXATION DATA

Taxation tables for personal tax – 2014/15

Note that 'TAXATION DATA 1' and 'TAXATION DATA 2' shown below will be available as pop up windows throughout your live assessment.

TAXATION DATA 1
Pop-up 1

Tax rates and bands

	%	£
Basic rate	20	first 31,865
Higher rate	40	to 150,000
Additional rate	45	over 150,000

Savings income is taxed at 10%, 20%, 40% and 45%
(10% applies to a maximum of £2,880 of savings income only where non-savings income is below this limit.)

Dividends are taxed at 10%, 32.5% and 37.5%.

Personal allowances

	£
Personal allowance for individuals born after 5 April 1948	10,000
Age allowance for individuals born between 6 April 1938 and 5 April 1948	10,500
Age allowance for individuals born before 6 April 1938	10,660
Income limit for age allowance	27,000

TAXATION DATA 2
Pop-up 2

Car benefit percentage

Emission rating for petrol engines	%
0g/km	0
1g/km to 75g/km	5
76g/km to 94g/km	11
95g/km or more	12% + 1% for every extra 5g/km above 95g/km

Diesel engines – additional 3%

The figure for fuel is £21,700

Authorised mileage rates

First 10,000 miles   45p
Over 10,000 miles   25p

Van scale charge

                            £
Charge   3,090
Private fuel provided   581

HMRC official rate   3.25%

Capital gains tax

Annual exempt amount   £11,000
Tax rate   18%
Higher rate   28%

Notes

Notes

Notes

Notes

Notes

Notes

Notes

Notes

Notes

Notes

Notes

Notes

Notes

Notes